Punchy Quips and Quotes for Today

E. C. McKenzie

BAKER BOOK HOUSE
Grand Rapids, Michigan

Copyright 1975 by
Baker Book House Company

ISBN: 0-8010-5979-8

Printed in the United States of America

- There is only one thing wrong with many human faces—they show!
- Almost everything comes to him who waits—including gray hair, false teeth, and a potbelly.
- Don't frown at the rain, it's the only thing that's coming down.
- Everything wears out sooner than it used to—including your nerves.
- Teen-age boys who whistle at girls are just going through a stage which will probably last fifty years.
- Some people have gear trouble. They talk in high and think in low.
- Last year, Marcus Welby, M.D., removed a man's gallbladder three different times within a period of eight months.
- He who laughs last usually has a tooth missing.
- Can you remember when drug abuse was merely another dose of castor oil?
- The house in which a man is the boss is probably still under construction.
- An expert on dairy herd management wrote that cows are sometimes bitter and neurotic. They're probably like a lot of taxpayers. They get tired of being milked.
- Sadder than falling leaves is falling hair.
- Bathing suits are really something—if you call nothing something.
- Sign in a delicatessen in Grand Rapids, Michigan, If You Can't Smell It—We Don't Have It.
- A hospital should have a recovery room adjoining the cashier's office.
- If you can express yourself clearly, you should be especially careful not to enter politics.
- An actress in Hollywood has broken up so many homes that she's listed in the Yellow Pages under "Demolition Experts."
- Some people have flat feet—and heads to match.
- Things are so tough these days that hitchhikers are willing to go either way.

- Isn't it strange how often small talk comes in such large doses?
- It's about time somebody invents a tax that can't be hiked.
- A man in Wisconsin says that if he went where people told him to go he'd be a man of great warmth.
- Don't bother telling people about your troubles. Half of them don't care, and the other half figure you probably have it coming to you.
- If there's always room at the top, why is there so much shoving going on up there?
- A pest is someone who goes out of his way to get in yours.
- Vodka is odorless, colorless, tasteless—and too much of it leaves you senseless.
- The most important thing in a relationship between a man and a woman is sincerity—whether you mean it or not.
- A window sign in Chicago, Tax Returns Prepared—Honest Mistakes Our Specialty.
- Can you remember when heartburn came from eating the meal, not from paying for it?
- Anybody who says this is a man's world is probably not too bright about other things either.
- The meanest man on earth is the fellow who gives a friend with loose dentures a piece of bubble gum.
- Some people's weakness is the strongest thing about them.
- About the only way a wife can keep her husband from looking at other women is to serve him wood alcohol.
- Don't forget the folks who are holding the ladder while you're climbing it to success.
- The difference between a radio and a clothesline is that one draws the waves and the other waves the drawers.
- A Kansas mother says her son's report card shows that he is courteous, prompt, attentive, cooperative, and dumb.
- There are two things that seem impossible to do—put toothpaste back in the tube and get off a mailing list.
- Some people pay their bills when due, some when overdue, and some never do.
- The best things in life are free—including the worst advice.
- A prominent gentleman in Dayton, Ohio, denies that he's conceited but says he's absolutely convinced that if he hadn't been born people would want to know why.

- Everything is changing so fast these days that even nostalgia isn't what it used to be.
- The best thing to put into a homemade pie is your teeth.
- Folks who tell all they know seldom stop there.
- If you've never seen a total eclipse, watch the groom at a wedding!
- Driving while drunk is almost as dangerous today as walking while sober.
- Even though most of us are married, life somehow must go on.
- An Indiana politician recently said, "I have many faults—but being wrong isn't one of them."
- Football isn't as violent as it appears—certainly not like trying to get to the rest rooms at half time!
- Don't you long for the good old days when Uncle Sam lived within his income and without most of yours?
- A small town is usually divided by a railroad, a main street, two churches, and a lot of opinions.
- You can't fool all the people all the time—some of them are fooling you.
- You're ready to leave the hospital when the food begins to taste good.
- A dance studio in Omaha is introducing a *politician's dance*. You take each step with caution.
- Why is it that the person who always says what he thinks has so many repulsive thoughts?
- With fuel shortages, inflation, and corruption in government, anybody who wishes you a happy New Year will probably lie about other things, too.
- It seems the less a fellow knows the more positive he is about it.
- A riot is what happens when a nonviolent demonstration meets a peaceful protest.
- What America needs most at the present time is a shortage of shortages.
- A woman's work is never done, especially if she asks her husband to do it.
- Almost everybody is in favor of a reasonable amount of law and order.
- An elderly lady in a cafeteria line sighed, "Why is it that everything I can afford is either chopped, ground, or smothered?"

- In the good old days, people stopped spending when they ran out of money.

- The top world leaders will all go down in history—some further down than others.

- If beauty-shop prices get much higher, it'll be cheaper to get a new wife than to have the old one done over.

- A Denver bachelor advertised for a wife in the newspaper, "Bachelor with water bed desires to meet a nice, hardworking girl with short toenails."

- Striker's picket sign, Time Heals All Wounds. Time and a Half Heals Them Faster.

- Did you hear about the cafe in San Francisco that had midget waiters so as to make the steaks look bigger?

- The best way to keep up with the Joneses is by correspondence.

- Nothing can make more noise than a man with asthma trying to eat celery.

- Which do you suppose ages faster—whiskey or the man who drinks it?

- A man complains about the food when he eats at home and about the prices when he eats out.

- When it comes to making use of food for thought, some folks stay on a hunger strike most of the time.

- A good friend is someone who can tell you all his problems —but doesn't.

- Why doesn't somebody come up with a tenderizer for people?

- Everything gets easier with practice—except getting out of bed in the morning.

- Diets are so strict nowadays that the only thing dieters are allowed to have is hunger pains.

- The best way to win an argument with a woman is to hit her over the head with a new mink coat.

- If you think some of the people at your class reunion look old and weather-beaten—think of those who didn't have the nerve to come.

- Any girl who knows how to cook can find a man who knows how to eat.

- There must be a lot of good in some people because very little of it ever comes out.

- Teen-age boys will drive anything—except a lawnmower.

- A henpecked husband washes the dishes—even when they use paper plates.

- Anyone who thinks he knows all the answers just isn't up to date on the questions.
- A shortage of popcorn is being predicted. That's terrible. Can you imagine going to the movies and being able to hear the dialogue!
- The only thing that goes faster than a teen-age driver is a five-dollar bill.
- You're not necessarily nuts if you talk to yourself—only if you listen.
- The hardest thing about climbing the ladder of success is getting through the crowd at the bottom.
- Just about the time you think you have everything in the bag, the bag busts.
- It's surprising how often people will agree with you if you just keep your mouth shut.
- A movie company made an X-rated western. Even the wagons weren't covered.
- Many of us make other folks look good simply by looking so bad ourselves.
- A typical bachelor's apartment has more dishes in the sink than on the shelves.
- Many a mouth is working overtime while the brain is on vacation.
- It is the man who has done nothing who is sure nothing can be done.
- A husband and wife are exactly alike in one respect—neither is able to fool the other for very long.
- Not since Indians collected scalps have so many people walked around with hair that's not their own.
- A bore never seems to have a previous engagement.
- It's getting to where things ain't cheap even at half-price.
- Rocking in a chair that doesn't creak is almost like being alone.
- Inflation is when everything at a dollar sale is marked $1.98.
- The first thing a man makes in his workshop is a mess.
- Unquestionably there is progress. The average American now pays out as much in taxes as he formerly got in wages.
- If it weren't for your conscience, you'd probably do anything you wanted to right away.
- A woman's best beauty aid is a nearsighted man.
- There are three kinds of traffic: urban, suburban, and bourbon.

- The worst thing about living in a mobile home is that there's no place to put anything except where it belongs.
- You'll never get to the top if you keep blowing yours.
- A man in Idaho reports that he has a drinking uncle who joined Alcoholics Anonymous but never attended meetings. He'd drink and send in the bottles.
- Men who found their way through the trackless wilderness now have great-grandsons who get lost in the supermarket.
- The kindest word in all the world is the unkind word, unsaid.
- There are no new sins—we just keep rerunning the old ones.
- If you're going around in circles, maybe it's because you're cutting too many corners.
- Any dieter will tell you that the one thing worse than a menu offering nothing you like is a menu offering everything you like.
- Political bumper stickers usually last longer than the politicians.
- A budget is an orderly way of discovering that you can't live on what you're earning.
- Youngsters always brighten up a home. They never turn out the lights.
- Withholding tax—instead of taking it out of your hide, they hide it out of your take.
- One advantage of today's high postal rates is that when you write a girl a love letter, she knows you mean it.
- Some men embrace their wives as if they're afraid of being penalized for holding.
- At today's food prices, the man who goes bankrupt can blame it on what he ate.
- There's a swank hospital so expensive that when you're brought in they interview you to see what diseases you can afford to have.
- Our next Thanksgiving menu will probably consist of roast turkey, yams, and pickled relatives.
- Los Angeles is a wonderful city. On a clear day when the fog lifts, you can see the smog.
- Being a go-getter is fine and dandy, but being an already-gotter is better.
- A girl will string along with a fellow long enough to see if he is fit to be tied.
- Some people go to a psychiatrist slightly cracked and leave completely broke.

- Keep your ear to the ground and you'll pick up a lot of dirt.
- Inflation is the nation's number one pickpocket.
- Installment loans have revolutionized our society. Never before have so many lived so far advanced while being so far behind.
- If you think time heals everything, try sitting in a doctor's office.
- America is achieving a high standard of poverty.
- If we are living in the lap of luxury, it may be we are on the last lap.
- The best way to beat the slot machine is with a hammer.
- There are two types of people who'll tell you there are better places to be than where you are—real-estate salesmen and preachers.
- These days, most of the meat-market beef comes from the customer's side of the counter.
- The world needs a new law that would prevent any country from waging war unless it pays for it in advance.
- Many people carefully avoid discovering the secret of success because deep down they suspect the secret may be *hard work.*
- Gossip is something that you must hurry to tell someone else before you find out it isn't true.
- Putting away something for a rainy day requires a longer stretch of fair weather than it used to.
- An injured professional football player in Chicago has begun working out and should be ready for TV commercials in a week or two.
- Money can still talk, but most of us can't hold on to it long enough to hear what it says.
- Any man who knows all the answers most likely misunderstood the questions.
- A midtown drug store in Houston is now selling a big bottle of aspirin for only forty-five cents and above it is a sign, Now You Can Afford to Treat the Headache Caused by Inflation.
- Daytime TV is the punishment inflicted on people who stay home when they're not really sick.
- Before you give somebody a piece of your mind, be sure you can get by with what you have left!
- Diplomacy may be defined as telling your boss he has an open mind instead of telling him he has holes in his head.
- A gentleman in Illinois says he didn't know he was involved in a computer marriage until he discovered his wife had a calculating mother.

- How to handle a bad temper: Be like a kettle—sing when you boil.
- There was a time when people ordered steak rare. Now they order steak rarely.
- The trouble with life is that by the time you know how to play the game, you're too old to make the team.
- More and more we realize what a great man Abraham Lincoln was. His face is found on pennies—we can't even get our hands on them.
- The best thing for gray hair is to keep it.
- Tact is the ability to stay in the middle without being caught there.
- You're never so much at a loss for words as when you put your foot in your mouth.
- When a woman listens to what her husband has to say, she's probably on the extension.
- Balance your budget—rotate your creditors.
- The trouble with our age is that it is all signposts and no destination.
- An old southern gentleman has a simple philosophy, Fill what's empty, empty what's full, and scratch where it itches.
- Sign at a railroad crossing near a country store in Georgia, Go Ahead—Take a Chance. We Buy Junk.
- One thing is certain, smiles never go up in price or down in value.
- Republicans think Santa Claus is a Democrat. So do Democrats.
- Before you have an argument with the boss, you'd better take a good look at both sides—his side and the outside.
- One trouble with TV is that a fellow has to wake up before he can go to bed.
- There are about as many people in this country who wear glasses as drink from them.
- Sound friendships are based less on sounds than on deeds.
- When a fellow starts trying to live within his means, folks wonder what else is wrong with him.
- Nowadays, just about everybody is putting his money where his mouth is—to kiss it good-bye.
- Politicians admit that the two-party system consists of the appointed and the disappointed.

- The biggest shortage of all is the common-sense shortage.
- Next Christmas Santa Claus certainly won't be the only guy in the red.
- Don't advertise your troubles; people are already oversupplied.
- It's amazing how a woman can know her husband inside out and never realize there's a button off his shirt.
- Thankfulness could well be the finest sentiment of man—and also the rarest.
- The trouble with a lot of people these days is they like to have their work cut out for them—completely.
- Unless you have never been tempted, don't pass judgment on someone who has yielded.
- The girl who used to wait for the right man to come along goes out these days looking for a fellow who's waiting for the right girl to come along.
- When a man sticks to his guns, you can be pretty sure they're loaded—or he is.
- Bumper sticker in Balitmore, Born Free—But Taxed to Death.
- A Miami husband asked his wife what she wanted for her birthday. She answered, "A long fur coat and a short football season."
- Many people never exercise except when sleeping and resting.
- After a long survey it has been discovered that there are three ages at which men misbehave—young, middle, and old.
- When a woman wants her husband to start a garden, the first thing he usually digs up is a good excuse.
- Capital punishment is when the government taxes your capital so that it can go into competition with you, and then taxes your profits to pay its losses.
- The trouble with being punctual is that, nine times out of ten, there is nobody there to appreciate it.
- For every judge operating in an official capacity, there are a hundred who are self-appointed.
- Any man who can get out of bed in the morning is in pretty good shape to start with. Ask any man who can't.
- The only break some people get these days is a coffee break.
- Since taking a speed-reading course, a man in Kentucky reports that he now seldom walks into the wrong rest room.
- Ad for an X-rated movie, For People over XXI.

- Another lethal weapon that isn't properly recognized as being dangerous is a wife with a credit card.
- Many an old settler had to settle down in the west because he couldn't settle up back east.
- Why should some people be willing to compromise when they're the ones who are always right?
- The best sense of humor belongs to the person who can laugh at himself.
- Our economy has gotten to the point where a counterfeiter can't even make a profit.
- The best exercise today is hunting for a bargain.
- It's too bad a shower of rain can't freshen up people like it does flowers and grass.
- A warranty is what expires just before the thing breaks down.
- A Texas cynic says people shouldn't marry on Sunday—because it's wrong to gamble on the Lord's Day.
- Conserve electric power! Share your electric blanket with a friend.
- The automobile is an invention which makes people go fast and money go faster.
- Some people have to moonlight just to see daylight.
- A Louisiana father wishes he hadn't made his son get a haircut. Now he can see his earrings.
- Something for nothing often costs too much.
- Those who have a right to boast don't need to.
- The grandfather who thought nothing about walking four miles to school is sure to have a grandson who doesn't think much of it either.
- Man's mind, stretched by a new idea, never goes back to its original dimensions.
- Forgive your enemies—if you can't get back at them any other way.
- A fellow can't keep folks from having a bad opinion of him, but he can keep them from being right about it.
- Sign over the front door of a big supermarket in Salt Lake City, Nobody Under $21 Admitted.
- Imagination was given to man to compensate him for what he is not, a sense of humor to console him for what he is.
- If Evel Knievel really wants to do something heroic, let him jump over some of those midtown potholes with his motorcycle.

- A class reunion is where everybody gets together to see who is falling apart.
- The reason more wives than husbands leave home is that few men know how to pack their own suitcases.
- Why not spend your vacation in Las Vegas? You can't beat the sunshine, the climate, or the slot machines.
- A bore is someone who is "me-deep" in conversation with no twinkle in his "I."
- Isn't it sneaky the way they call it a "tax return"—as if your money was going to make a round trip!
- A North Carolina wife says her husband is a great athlete. He can hang over a bar and chin for hours.
- The trouble with pulling the wool over the voter's eyes is that they soon recognize the yarn.
- Some banks guarantee maximum interest for four years —which is more than a marriage license can do.
- Taking off weight is good for your health, your appearance, and your tailor.
- An amazing thing about a man being arrested for disturbing the peace these days is that he found any.
- When old-timers were kids, they were lucky to have wall-to-wall floors.
- There seems to be too much political jam on the relief rolls.
- About all some people want out of life is a little unfair advantage.
- Women are usually busy rearranging their faces, their furniture, or their figures.
- Someone said to a man who had led in public prayer, "You should speak louder. I didn't hear a word you said." His reply was, "I wasn't talking to you."
- If you wish to appear agreeable in society, you must be content to be taught many things you already know.
- Controlling inflation without causing a depression is equivalent to sticking a pin into a balloon gradually.
- A concert pianist in Cleveland claims he's doing his part to conserve energy. He's now playing the piano with only one hand.
- Nowadays it seems that everything is divided into two parts —what you don't like and what you can't afford.
- There's a new diet that includes tranquilizers. You don't lose much weight—but you really don't care.

- If it weren't for giving directions, some people wouldn't get any exercise at all.
- Success in life depends more on push than pull.
- It's difficult for a fellow to have much faith in God if he has too much in himself.
- *Automation* is a process that gets all the work done while you just sit there. When we were growing up this process was called *mother*.
- Giving good advice does not qualify as charity.
- An eighty-two-year-old gentleman in New Orleans recently remarked, "At my age I still chase girls—but only if it's downhill."
- Among many others, there is this one important difference between men and women—women are smarter than men about women.
- The nice thing about money is that it never clashes with anything you're wearing.
- Many people think they have an open mind, when it's really their mouth.
- "Almost right" is still wrong.
- A vacation makes you feel good enough to go back to work and so poor, you have to.
- The biggest difference between right and wrong is that folks are usually wrong more times than they are right.
- A soap opera is where it takes a woman eleven months to have a premature baby.
- The "radical left" says it will work within the system. So do termites!
- No man ever convinced his wife that a pretty secretary is as efficient as a homely one.
- Some people nowadays buy a new car with one down payment and thirty-five *darn* payments.
- A New Mexico housewife suspects her butcher is using phony scales. She said, "Last week I didn't buy anything at the meat market—and it weighed three pounds."
- Nothing makes advice seem so helpful as giving it.
- A miracle is a flower that turns out as pretty as the seed catalogue pictured it.
- Sign in a waiting room of a maternity ward in Birmingham, "Call Us Any Time of Day or Night. We Deliver.
- It's reached the point where economy costs a lot more than it once did.

- An old-timer remembers when a family that couldn't afford to own a car didn't.

- Many people are not exactly stingy—they're just economical in a very obnoxious way.

- In some parts of Africa, a man doesn't know his wife until he marries her—but why single out Africa?

- There's a shortage of doctors everywhere in this country except on TV.

- We're thankful that we have free speech here in America—and equally thankful that there's no law requiring us to listen to it.

- The only consolation about higher grocery prices is that we get more trading stamps.

- When they say he was a "born executive," they mean that his father owned the business.

- Mrs. Josephine Honeyfunkle of Dallas was recently honored at a country-club dinner party for her forty-sixth birthday. She had been a resident of Dallas for fifty-seven years.

- In national politics, it's not how you play the game as much as it is who's keeping score.

- Cosmetics were used in the Middle Ages; in fact, they're still used in the middle ages.

- If you don't think the dollar is worth anything today, just try to collect a few of them from your debtors.

- Marriage often results when a man meets a woman who understands him. So does divorce.

- A guaranteed annual income is nothing new in this country. We've had alimony for many years.

- Isn't it wonderful to have such a beautiful world to suffer in?

- It takes all kinds of people to make a world—but it seems as if the world would be a lot better off if it didn't.

- A boaster and a liar are first cousins.

- There's one thing desperately wrong with our country—too many folks are earning their bread by the sweat of the taxpayer's brow.

- It's getting so that take-home pay can hardly survive the trip.

- Some American wives have found a blackmail device to get their husbands to take them out to dinner. They threaten to cook.

- Middle age is when your legs buckle—and your belt doesn't.

- The big question is: Where can we put our hatred while we say our prayers?

- Everything is getting so high these days that the newest addition to shortages is money.
- A "dirty old man" is one with two teen-age daughters and one bathroom.
- Nursing a grudge is like arguing with a policeman—the more you do, the worse things get.
- A small town in Georgia is so far ahead of the times that it has a Fifth Day Adventist Church.
- On the average, people who hurry through life get through it quicker.
- Retirement can be a great joy if you can figure out how to spend time without spending money.
- An opera is a place where anything that's too dumb to be spoken is sung.
- A filibuster is when a senator talks a long time without saying anything—as usual.
- Many people will never be bothered by air pollution because they don't stop talking long enough to take a deep breath.
- *Etc.* is a sign used to make people think you know more than you do.
- These are days when we wish newscasters would cast their news somewhere else.
- To be sure of hitting the target, shoot first and whatever you hit—call it the target.
- The best time to miss a train is at a crossing.
- A husband is never as good as his wife thought he was before marriage and never as bad as she thinks him to be after marriage.
- To be thought wise, keep your mouth shut.
- In covering the subject, don't smother it.
- Dedicated ignorance gets you nowhere.
- Things aren't like they used to be—including you.
- A "moderately-good Christian" is like a "moderately-good egg."
- The first screw to loosen in the human body is the one that controls the tongue.
- Save yourself trouble by not borrowing any.
- Old taxes never die—they just change their names.
- Blowing your stack adds to air pollution.

- It's easier to float rumors than to sink them.
- Wise men admit their mistakes, fools defend their mistakes.
- If experience is the best teacher, many of us are pretty poor pupils.
- Sign in the window of a flower shop, We Don't Mind If You Stick Your Nose in Our Business.
- It's all right to be dumb, but it's stupid to make a career out of it.
- Whatever became of the term *popular prices*?
- Who will be the modern Moses to lead us out of the bewilderment?
- Can you remember when movies used to boast of being in technicolor instead of off-color?
- It was either the late Will Rogers or an old maid who said, "I never met a man I didn't like."
- Most of us are just like we were thirty years ago—only in slow motion.
- When Eskimos meet they rub noses—Americans rub fenders.
- Almost everybody is growing five things in the garden this year—peas, radishes, beans, tomatoes, and tired.
- Bumper sticker on a 1950-model car, When Passing, Watch Out for Flying Parts.
- There are fleeting moments when everything seems to be going along very well; don't worry, it won't last.
- Nowadays when a woman phones her husband to stop in at the cleaners, she isn't referring to the dry cleaner—she means the supermarket.
- Often our mistakes serve a useful purpose. Our friends find much pleasure in pointing them out to us.
- The mind is a wonderful thing—everybody should have one.
- If the service rendered by the United States Postal Department ever gets worse—how will we know it?
- A cynic in South Carolina says if he could get back his membership fee, he'd resign from the human race.
- An old-timer is one who can remember when a girl with hidden charms hid them.
- Money isn't everything, but it's a pretty good cure for poverty.
- With some people, a clear conscience is nothing more than a poor memory.
- So far, banana and snake oil are still plentiful.

- A little learning is a dangerous thing—but it still beats total ignorance.
- One thing a woman doesn't often find in her purse is whatever she's looking for.
- If the good Lord had intended for us to live in a permissive society, wouldn't the Ten Commandments have been the Ten Suggestions?
- If swimming is good for the figure, how do you account for the whale?
- Many people today are suffering from the paralysis of analysis.
- The honeymoon is over when the bride begins to suspect that she was never anything to him but a tax deduction.
- A sale is a merchandising event in which everything is reduced in price except the item you want to buy.
- Everybody should communicate with one another—it can't make things any worse.
- You'll never get anywhere else if you don't leave where you are now.
- The trouble with living it up is that you may never live it down.
- A doctor in Philadelphia advised a hypochondriac patient, "Just drink plenty of liquids, get lots of rest, and stop watching Marcus Welby."
- Time separates the best of friends. So does money—and don't forget marriage.
- Sign outside a church building in Boston, All New Sermons —No Reruns.
- Abraham Lincoln wasn't a handsome man, but he looks mighty good on a five-dollar bill.
- Some people who try to look casual end up looking accidental.
- Those who can, do. Those who can't, aren't trying.
- The longer we live, the less future there is to worry about.
- A green salesman can sell more than a blue one.
- It may be true that bachelors make more mistakes than married men—but they don't make the big one.
- There's a new drink on the market called FOREIGNADE. It's the refreshment that never pauses.
- There are only two kinds of egotists—those who admit it and the rest of us.
- It's peculiar how much longer it takes folks to say what they think than to tell what they know.

- The United States is running out of things our grandfathers never imagined anybody would need.
- If life were a bed of roses, some people wouldn't be happy until they developed an allergy.
- Some folks look ahead, some look back, but most look worried.
- It would be extremely nice if there were as many new ways of making money as there are of spending it.
- A doctor in Albuquerque is doing so well financially that he can occasionally tell a patient there is nothing wrong with him.
- Darwin's theory of evolution suggests that first came the baboon and then man. Politics is proving that it can go either way.
- An example of progress is the fact that every year it takes less time and more money to get you where you're going.
- If you want to know what's wrong with a candidate—elect him!
- When you find that things start to get blurred, get stronger glasses—or weaker drinks.
- Yesterday is past history—except when it is taped.
- If you're not an adult when you go to see a movie these days, you are when you come out.
- Liberty doesn't work as well in practice as it does in speeches.
- It's paradoxical that the thicker a person's skull, the more likely he is to blow his top.
- The best time to start thinking about your retirement is before the boss does.
- There is a close relationship between getting up in the world and getting up in the morning.
- At today's prices, it costs almost as much to go through a checkout counter as through college.
- The automobile is the most destructive plaything man has ever known.
- *Divorce* is nothing more than the past tense of marriage.
- You will never know what is enough unless you know what's more than enough.
- For every person who brags about being bright, there are a dozen ready to polish him off.
- Keep your chin up, but not to the point where your nose is in the air.
- We demand college degrees for those who teach our children—with no requirement for those who rear them.

- People will believe almost anything they think they weren't supposed to hear.
- Nothing seems to make the cost of living so reasonable as pricing funerals.
- Once a man learns to listen, he can stay on speaking terms with his wife indefinitely.
- *Consultation* is a medical term meaning share the wealth.
- If some folks aren't careful, they'll stretch their coffee break clear to the unemployment office.
- We have come from somewhere and we are going somewhere. The Great Architect of the universe never built a stairway that leads nowhere.
- One possible reason why things aren't going according to plan is that there never was a plan.
- A Nevada husband complains that there are two reasons why his wife won't wear last year's dresses. She doesn't want to —and she can't.
- Even with the price of everything going up, writing paper remains *stationery*.
- A great deal of what we see depends on what we're looking for.
- The straight and narrow path has never been closed for repairs.
- Sometimes a movie is so bad you're sorry you asked the woman in front of you to remove her hat.
- There's a lot to be said for not saying a lot.
- Many people have lost the way to happiness in the search for pleasure.
- There's a popular bachelor in Nebraska who has the reputation of continually running after women. Last year he caught one.
- It has been said that the world is a stage. It might be added that lately a great many amateurs have been hogging the spotlight.
- A perfectionist is a person who takes enough pain to give everybody else one.
- It's called *take-home pay* because there's no other place you can afford to go with it.
- Independence Day, to an ever increasing number of Americans, is the day their divorce becomes final.
- The object of political primaries is to choose a promiser who'll out-promise the other party's promiser.
- Money is what things run into and folks are running out of these days.

- Among the most popular remedies that won't cure a cold is advice.
- Any man who can't laugh at his own joke is probably married to a woman who has just messed it up.
- If you steal from one author, that's *plagiarism*; if you steal from twenty authors, that's *research*!
- We are all ready to vote a straight ticket next election—as soon as we can find out which party is straight.
- The best way to enjoy a beautiful, productive garden is to live next door to one and cultivate your neighbor.
- Ever since a certain president of the United States gave all his salary back to the government, the idea caught on—and now they've got us all doing it.
- Many men are now reporting that payday at their house is like the Academy Awards. Their wives say, "May I have the envelope, please?"
- The person who gives you free advice is probably charging you too much for it.
- Most of us can make ends meet. What we'd like to do is to make them overlap a little.
- Before proceeding with any difficult task, stop and think. Then remember to start again.
- You have reached middle age when a night out is followed by a day in.
- A censor is a guy why finds three meanings in a joke that has only two.
- Nowadays when you talk about a man who stands head and shoulders above the crowd you probably mean some high-priced basketball star.
- Lettered on the back of a school bus, Approach with Care—Driver Under the Influence of Children.
- A child's definition of a torture chamber is a living room or den without a TV set.
- Hard work never killed anybody, but some of us sure don't want to take a chance on being the first victim.
- It's surprising how easy it is for a man to understand a woman—when he's not married to her.
- Plan ahead—it wasn't raining when Noah built the ark.
- Postal rates have gone up again—which means we are getting more of a licking than the stamps do.

- Many grandmothers didn't use mascara or nail polish when they were girls—but they do now.
- The most difficult thing an after-dinner speaker has to learn is not to nod while the toastmaster is praising him.
- It was so much easier when there was just good and bad. Today there are too many options in between.
- Far too frequently in this life we are interested in only three persons: me, myself, and I.
- Some tasks have to be put off dozens of times before they will completely slip the mind.
- A good way to get your name in the newspaper is to cross the street reading one.
- Some people only open their mouth when they have nothing to say.
- Nothing is harder for a new driver to park than both ends of a car.
- Parents are embarrassed when their children tell lies, but sometimes it's even worse when they tell the truth.
- A chef is a man with a vocabulary so extensive and colorful that it enables him to give the soup a different name everyday.
- Some people who claim to be working their fingers to the bone are simply scratching their heads.
- A man doesn't know the value of a woman's love until he starts paying alimony.
- It seems like some people can't be happy unless they are unhappy.
- Sign in a supermarket in Nashville, Wanted—Clerk to Work Eight Hours a Day to Replace One Who Didn't.
- Courtship is that period during which the female decides whether or not she can do any better.
- Do something unusual today: *listen*.
- A psychiatrist's couch is where you land when you go off your rocker.
- Money is a thing you'd get along without beautifully if only other people weren't so crazy about it.
- At a party you can always tell which woman is a man's wife. She is the one for whom he doesn't turn on his marvelous smile.
- The only person who gladly listens to both sides of a family argument is the woman in the next apartment.
- Some doctors tell their patients the bad news man to man, others prefer to send the bill by mail.

- Your home town is the place where people wonder how you ever got as far as you did.
- The misinformed always know too much.
- People who brag about having an open mind should close it once in a while and think.
- There's only one thing wrong with $5.00 steaks in Chicago —they cost $9.50.
- Cheer up! At least thermometers are going down.
- Increasing taxes to stop inflation makes about as much sense as fanning a fire to cool its heat.
- A dentist in Little Rock claims the best collector of old bills is a new toothache.
- Economists predict the year ahead will reward hard workers. What a frightening outlook for many!
- A saver is a farsighted person who lays money away for the government's rainy day.
- Many a husband comes home from work and hopes the kitchen stove is as warm as the TV set.
- Some people know a lot more when you try to tell them something than when you ask them something.
- Many Americans are trying to conserve energy as never before—they're burning their morning toast only on one side.
- Sign outside a suburban shop in San Antonio, Don't Go Downtown to Be Robbed. Come Here.
- Anybody who's written his autobiography learns you make two kinds of enemies with such a book—the people you mention and those you don't.
- If you can't think of a snappy retort, a carefully concealed yawn is often as good and much less dangerous.
- A husband in Iowa reports that his wife lets him smoke his cigars in a special room—the garage.
- Be happy when your troubles are at their worst—it means that anything that happens will be an improvement.
- The increased load on city buses is so great that even some men have to stand up.
- You're not really successful till someone brags they sat beside you in grade school.
- Seat belts in automobiles are not as confining as wheel chairs.
- There are several things that money can't buy—among them is the same stuff it bought last week.

- Discretion is the fine art of forgiving your enemies—especially those you can't whip.
- The average householder gets so many sales letters telling him he has been selected that it's hard for him to stay humble.
- A New Year's resolution is a promise to stop doing everything you enjoy most.
- Many people aren't particular how you treat them—just as long as you do.
- The most difficult of all musical instruments to learn to play is second fiddle.
- It's a curious world when you can be in a jam one time and in a pickle another time and never know the difference.
- The man who thinks the world owes him a living is up against it when you ask him for an itemized statement.
- In middle age it's sometimes difficult to decide what there's most of—middle or age.
- There's nothing faster on a takeoff than a bus you've just missed.
- Sometimes a man who tells you he has a model wife might be easily tempted into looking over the later models.
- The prices are now so high that one book store in Minneapolis moved its cookbooks into the fantasy and science fiction section.
- Some restaurants are now serving energy-saving cocktails —drink two and the lights go out.
- The cart in the supermarket is rapidly becoming the most expensively operated vehicle in the world.
- Some people's mouths work faster than their brains. They say things they haven't even thought of yet.
- There's only one perfect child in the world and every mother has it.
- It isn't the cost of a strapless gown—it's the upkeep.
- Credit cards have made buying easier but paying harder.
- One disadvantage of being unemployed is that a person has no payday to borrow money until.
- Many young men would like to become dentists, but they don't seem to have enough pull.
- There's a new alarm clock for actors. It doesn't ring—it applauds.

- An Alabama husband recently remarked, "I'm concerned about my wife; she no longer nags with the same dedication she used to."
- Sign in a automobile show window in Phoenix, Let's All Fight Poverty Together. Buy a New Car.
- Rising costs don't bother the town drunk. He's been living high for years.
- A back-seat driver never runs out of gas.
- Modern science is simply wonderful. It would take fifty people working twenty years to make the same mistakes a computer can make in only two seconds.
- It's easy to milk a cow. Any jerk can do it.
- Despite all the pain and trouble, life is still better than any alternative.
- It can be dangerous for a husband to come home late at night—especially if he promised his wife he'd be home early.
- The guy who invented the boomerang is probably the same one who invented the credit card.
- They tell us that music isn't always as bad as it sounds.
- If you want to appreciate what an enormous job it is to clean up the environment, start by cleaning out your garage.
- The only thing some people pay is attention.
- Man is never so hard of hearing as when his opinions are being challenged.
- One nice thing about glass houses—no one can nail your hide to the wall.
- Too many are prone to let George do it and then complain about how he did it.
- A man in Oklahoma admitted he lied on his income tax return—he listed himself as the head of his household.
- Once upon a time when you felt the need for a good cry, you went to the movies; later soap operas did it—now it's the supermarket.
- Keeping a secret requires the ability to remember to forget what was told you.
- Fashion experts tell us that women dress to express themselves—but on that basis, some have very little to say.
- Nothing can relieve the pain of truth.

- To err is human, but if a fellow is smart he ought to think up a better excuse than that.
- There appears to be no more popular pastime these days than going off cigarettes—unless it's going back on them.
- The international situation is now as shifty as an armful of coat hangers.
- Marriage is somewhat like horseradish. Men praise it with tears in their eyes.
- A politician recently announced that he perfectly understands the questions of the day. The trouble is, he doesn't know the answers.
- Some people live simply because they want to. Others simply live because they have nothing else to do.
- An optimist is a boy who hurries because he thinks his date is ready and waiting for him.
- Those who feel Americans don't get enough exercise will probably be happy to know that there's been a revival in the use of snuff.
- There is a rapid change during a youth's adolesence. For instance, between fourteen and seventeen a parent can age twenty years.
- A friend is one who joyfully sings with you when you are on the mountain top and silently walks beside you through the valley.
- You never have to take a dose of your own medicine if you know when to keep your mouth shut.
- The first thing to turn green in the spring is the Christmas jewelry.
- No patient should leave the hospital until he's strong enough to face the cashier.
- A neck is something which, if you don't stick it *out*, you won't get into trouble *up to*.
- An old-timer is one who can remember when four or five teenagers could get together without forming a rock group.
- Sign in an Atlanta restaurant, Why Not Smile? It's the Only Thing You Can Wear That Isn't Taxed.
- Some wives know their husband's jokes backwards—and tell them that way.
- To make mistakes is human; to stumble is commonplace; to be able to laugh at yourself is maturity.
- An adolescent is a youth old enough to dress himself if he could just remember where he dropped his clothes.

- The average husband brings his wife flowers when he wants her to remember an event—or forget one.

- Give crabgrass an inch and it'll take a yard.

- The trouble with TV is that we sit watching the twenty-one-inch screen so much that we develop a twenty-inch bottom.

- Two-thirds of our population now live in big cities, the other third on the expressways.

- Today's dollar doesn't go very far—just beyond reach.

- The man who first said "spend" your vacation never knew how right he was.

- There is one good thing about our postal service. A lot of letters we wish we hadn't written are delivered long after anyone cares.

- Marriage will never become obsolete. Something is always happening that we can't blame on the government.

- Politics is almost as exciting as war and equally as dangerous. In war you can only be killed once, but in politics many times.

- If you have someone eating out of your hand, it's still a good idea to count your fingers at intervals.

- Something has to be done about food prices before eating becomes a spectator sport.

- Some of the older generation's criticism of the younger generation is heavily tinged with envy.

- When you learn a new skill, make a complete job of it. For instance, don't learn to swim halfway across the lake.

- There is little doubt that no freedom is so outrageously and so often abused as the freedom of speech.

- Few women seem to believe what their mirrors and bathroom scales tell them.

- A news item from a Denver newspaper, "Miss Mary Barnes of Tulsa, Oklahoma, a belle of twenty summers, is visiting her twin brother, age thirty-two."

- There are so many men who can figure costs, and so few who can measure values.

- With telephone rates due to go up again, we begin to wonder if what we have to say is still worth saying!

- The trouble with some after-dinner speakers is that they have a two-minute idea and a two-hour vocabulary.

- There are two kinds of people: those who think there are two kinds of people and those who think it's not that simple.

- A new TV set has been invented that automatically dispenses an aspirin tablet just before the six o'clock news comes on.
- By the time a fellow realizes what a drip he's been, it's too late to fix the faucet.
- A goal isn't worth much if you must lower it to reach it.
- Many a husband has learned that an ironclad alibi isn't as effective as a diamond-studded one.
- What's needed in Washington is an immunization against "staff" infection.
- Honesty gives a man strength but not always popularity.
- The wages of sin is death—shouldn't you quit before payday?
- You will probably find the key to success under your alarm clock.
- A hothead is one who is always blowing off steam.
- Wisdom lies in believing only half of what you hear; genius lies in knowing which half to believe.
- It's sad to realize that twenty years from now all of today's beautiful young women will be five years older.
- Children are innocent and love justice, while many adults are wicked and prefer mercy.
- A puzzle to any new camper is how the Arab folded his tent.
- Divorce illustrates the belief that united we stand—but divided we can stand better.
- The chronic liar always starts the same way, "They say. . . ."
- Political commercials on TV prove one thing—some candidates can tell you all their good points and qualifications in thirty seconds.
- Nobody wants the man who gives himself away.
- There's a new invention on the market—a pencil with an eraser on both ends. It's for people who do nothing but make mistakes.
- About the only thing you can get for a nickel nowadays is heads or tails.
- No drinker of booze ever takes more than one drink at a time.
- The man who sings his own praises may have the right tune but the wrong words.
- Medical science has yet to develop an ailment which will interest friends and neighbors as much as a black eye.

- There's a new outfit called Skier's Anonymous. If you feel like skiing, you just call them and they'll send someone over to break your leg.
- The old-fashioned mother who used to have prunes every morning now has a granddaughter who has dates every night.
- Making friends comes under several recipes, but the best formula is to be one yourself.
- A hypochondriac in Montgomery, Alabama, nervously asked her doctor, "Doc, I'm feeling fine today. What's that a symptom of?"
- Too many folks want to build a better world while acting in a foreman's capacity.
- About the time a man gets to thinking he's a big shot, somebody fires him.
- It's odd how temptation always seems to get action quicker than do good intentions.
- Just because you take a bath in private, don't think for a minute the public can't tell whether you've had one.
- A minor operation is one somebody else had.
- Why is it that the average wife seldom talks to her husband except when he's reading?
- A mere job becomes a "position" when the title is bigger than the salary.
- And there was the poor old man who worried so much about his bills that his hair began to fall out of his wig.
- About the only thing that's free of charge these days is a run-down battery.
- Sign on the front gate of a home in Florida, We Are Vegetarians, but Our Dog Isn't.
- If you get a good education, you can become prosperous if you marry a rich widow.
- With today's inflation, it's a question as to which is more costly—investing in the stock market or shopping in a supermarket.
- What this country needs is more fishing poles and fewer saxophones.
- Most of us are willing to give a fellow a helping hand if he'd only pick a more convenient time to need it.
- On his fiftieth wedding anniversary, a husband in Arkansas

explained his happy marriage, "At home I rule the roost—and my wife rules the rooster."

◇ Nowadays, there's only one thing wrong with money—poor circulation!

◇ Keep your teen-age daughter out of hot water—put dirty dishes in it.

◇ These days there are two kinds of people cutting down on food—those who can't afford the calories and those who can't afford the prices.

◇ A toy store in San Francisco has a doll house for $1200. It comes completely equipped—it even has its own mortgage.

◇ As a general rule, politics is a dirty business, but you can sure clean up in it.

◇ You can always depend on a bore doing the completely expected.

◇ A little pride is a small thing to lose when compared with losing honor.

◇ Sometime in the future somebody is going to invent a mirror that is willing to lie—and he's going to make himself a fortune.

◇ When a Texas school class was told that the next day they would learn to *draw*—eighteen youngsters showed up with pistols.

◇ Everybody should be paid what he's worth—no matter how much of a cut in salary he has to take.

◇ Sign in a church in Miami: Come to Church Next Sunday. If You Don't Have Any Sins—Bring Someone Who Has.

◇ The typical inferiority complex in Washington results from not having a telephone worth tapping.

◇ Maybe it's impolite to walk out of a party, but it's better that way than to stay and have to be carried out.

◇ Kindness is the ability to treat your enemy decently.

◇ When old-timers were kids, they thought a film was obscene if the horse wasn't wearing a saddle.

◇ The time is coming when the American people will elect two presidents—one for the White House and one for the road.

◇ It's a great kindness to entrust people with a secret. They feel so important while telling it to their friends.

◇ The trouble with not having prejudices is that people are apt to think you don't understand our social system.

- A spinster in Michigan complained, "Every time I meet a man who'd make a good husband—he already is."

- Most folks seem to want the right to worship as they wish—and to make others worship the same way.

- Don't be afraid to talk to yourself. It's the only way you can be sure somebody's listening.

- The pessimist grumbles because God put thorns on roses; the optimist thanks God that He put roses on thorns.

- There is nothing harder on the shins than soccer, unless, of course, it's bridge.

- The triumph song of life would lose its melody without its minor keys.

- Any girl can tell you that the only thing harder than a diamond is getting one.

- A "slight tax increase" costs you $300, while a "substantial tax cut" lowers your tax by $30.

- Child psychology is what parents often use to misunderstand their children.

- The people of the United States do not need more judges, rather more judgment.

- No man becomes either very good or very bad suddenly.

- In two days, tomorrow will be yesterday.

- Quarrels would not last very long if the fault were only on one side.

- Nothing makes a woman's clothes go out of style faster than her husband's raise in salary.

- After-dinner speeches can make you feel dumb at one end and numb on the other.

- In some foreign countries girls dress like their mothers, but in America it's the other way around.

- A class reunion is a gathering where you come to the conclusion that most of the people your own age are a lot older than you are.

- Education is a good thing, but it doesn't go far enough. It merely teaches a man *how* to speak, not *when* or *how long*. And neither does it teach him exactly when to shut up!

- About the only thing you can save from your pay envelope is the envelope.

- At today's food prices the dinner *hour* has been cut to about twenty minutes.
- Some people have presence of mind; others absence of thought.
- If it is true that we are approaching a moneyless society, some of us are ahead of our time.
- Friends are like a priceless treasure; he who has none is a social pauper.
- Some kids are like ketchup bottles—you have to slap their bottom a few times to keep them moving.
- Automobiles are a great deal like men—the less substantial they are, the more knocking they do.
- After four or five years on the sea of matrimony, many a wife notices something has gone out of her marriage. Usually it's her husband.
- Politicians are like ships. The more they encounter, the noisier they become.
- Relatively speaking, different levels of income use different terminology. The poor people have *kinsfolk*; the middle-class families have *relatives*; and the wealthy have *heirs*.
- If the knocking at the door is loud and long, it isn't opportunity. It's relatives.
- Anybody who stands on dignity isn't going anywhere.
- In June, road maps replace the May catalogues.
- The only walk more expensive than a walk down a church aisle is a walk down a supermarket aisle.
- What's all this talk about getting rich the hard way? Is there any other way?
- A freeloader never turns down an invitation—even when he doesn't get one.
- Sign in a small Oklahoma restaurant, Don't Complain About Our Waitress. She Has an Energy Crisis.
- Chivalry is opening the door and standing aside so some female can rush in and take the job you're after.
- Have you ever thought that you're not learning anything when you're doing all the talking?
- The odds on a diet succeeding are three to one against you —knife, fork, and spoon.
- Forget about attending school and nobody will be wiser —especially you.

- A hangover is when you don't want to come out of your room because you think your head won't fit through the door.

- Attention wives: If your husband complains about the tie you gave him for Christmas—give him a sock!

- A North Dakota gentleman complains that he can't keep up with the new styles. He said that just when long hair became stylish, his started to fall out.

- This electronic age has its drawbacks. Parents who once showed you their kids' pictures now bore you with their tape recorders.

- Politicians are poor tippers—they're not as careless with their money as they are with ours.

- Nowadays, anyone who puts two and two together also has to add in the sales tax.

- There's a new drive-in theater in Indianapolis for married couples only. No necking in the back seat—just arguing.

- Today's temper tantrum is tomorrow's anti-establishment demonstration.

- You can't expect a person to see eye to eye with you when you're looking down on him.

- Most people are interested in the higher things in life these days—such as salaries.

- A fifth-grade youngster reported to his father that he was almost at the top of the list of those that flunked.

- You're an old-timer if you can remember when the village square was a place instead of a person.

- The happiest people are those who are too busy to notice whether they are or not.

- A store with a Going Out Of Business sign added another, We Reserve the Right to Stay in Business If This Sale Is a Success.

- The couple who years ago walked out of a movie because it was dirty now has a grandchild who walks out because it isn't.

- A Florida cynic complains that when a woman changes her mind, it doesn't work any better than the old one.

- If you had it all to do over, would you fall in love with yourself again?

- The height of politeness is to listen with interest to things you know about, from someone who doesn't.

- A bore is one who keeps you from being lonely, but makes you wish you were.

- Members of Congress meet more often than they get together.
- When a coward is in trouble, he always thinks of his legs first.
- Old age is when it takes you longer to get over a good time than to have it.
- If a man looks at a woman, it doesn't necessarily mean he's interested in her. Still, a man seldom looks at a road map unless he's planning to go somewhere.
- Sad but true—money and hair seem important only when you no longer have any.
- The reason it's later than some people think is that they can't think as fast as time passes by.
- We simply can't understand why folks who don't know whether they are coming or going are always in such a hurry to get there.
- Sign on a Hollywood car, Just Remarried.
- The way some people sound off on news, you'd think the daily paper printed only one copy, and they had it.
- It was so cold in Washington last winter that a politician was seen with his hands in his own pockets.
- The distance to the moon used to be measured in miles, now it's in dollars.
- Behind every successful man is another man who claims he went to school with him.
- The man with a new idea is considered a crank until the idea succeeds.
- Gypsies deserve a lot of credit. Who else, in these times, would have the nerve to look into the future?
- Skiing is a colorful sport—plenty of white snow and Blue Cross.
- If you can't think of any other way to flatter a man, tell him he's the kind of man who can't be flattered.
- Almost everything comes to those who wait; but when they come, they're out of date.
- If you look back too much, you will soon be headed that way.
- A beautiful heart seems to transform a homely face.
- Just over the hill is a beautiful valley, but you must climb the hill to see it.
- Nowadays some people only feel good when their pep pills forge ahead of their tranquilizers.
- Women are very secretive about their age, but they'll gladly tell their husbands how old their fur coats are.
- You can't learn very much by listening to yourself all the time.

- A foolish opinion shared by many thousands is still a foolish opinion.
- If you did today all that you had planned, maybe you didn't plan enough.
- An economist is a man who figures out tomorrow why the things he predicted yesterday didn't happen today.
- The sale of electric guitars should be banned for at least two years. This would not only conserve electricity, it would also eliminate a lot of noise pollution.
- A true friend is one who is thinking of you when all others are thinking of themselves.
- Freedom also includes the right to mismanage your own affairs.
- It's easy to understand human nature when we bear in mind that almost everybody thinks he's as exception to most rules.
- A successful man keeps on looking for work after he has found a job.
- Opportunity usually knocks but once, and that may be the reason it has a better reputation than other knockers.
- A child has reached the awkward age when he begins to ask questions that have answers.
- Television is a wonderful thing—you can sit at home any evening, relax, and watch your wife's favorite shows.
- Most girls are very romantic. They expect a declaration of love to have a ring in it.
- If life was a bowl of cherries, chances are two to one that the pickers would go on strike.
- Politics is the science of how who gets what, when, and why.
- Waiting for some people to stop talking is like looking for the end of a roller towel.
- A man who seldom takes more than one drink explained, "One drink is just right; two is too many; and three is not enough."
- Last year wasn't too bad; but if it had been manufactured, it would have likely been recalled.
- Quite a number of boys in New Orleans asked to be excused from school the day of the senior prom. They wanted to have their hair done.
- It takes most men about two years to completely quit smoking cigarettes and twice as long to quit bragging about it.
- In Hollywood a marriage is considered a success if the groom carries the bride all the way across the threshold.

- Nowadays the words, "Early to bed and early to rise" probably mean the TV is busted.
- Having no food to eat will take your mind off other troubles.
- Epitaph on a tombstone in Arizona, I Expected This, but Not Just Yet.
- Nothing stretches quite as far as a campaign promise.
- Wearing shorts usually reveals as much about a man's indifference to public opinion as it does anything else.
- Anybody who thinks there must be fire where there's smoke has never tried burning autumn leaves.
- Before you criticize a man for allowing grass to grow under his feet, you ought to find out if his power mower is out of order.
- Children are unpredictable. You never know when they're going to catch you in a lie.
- Life is like a game of poker—if you don't put any in the pot, there won't be any to take out.
- Careful grooming may make you look twenty years younger, but it still won't fool a flight of stairs.
- It's not what you look at that counts every time—but what you see.
- Modern man meets a crisis face to face—after taking a pill.
- Never judge a summer resort by its postcards.
- To talk without saying anything is worse than silence.
- A New Jersey woman complains that it's been so long since her husband took a good look at her that if anything happened he wouldn't be able to identify the body.
- Looking into the mirror isn't usually the best way to convince yourself that certain things are improving.
- Most of us are broad-minded enough to admit that there are two sides to every question—our own side and the side that no intelligent, informed, sane, and self-respecting citizen could possibly hold.
- The way apartments are made nowadays, you can get to know all about your neighbors before you even meet them.
- When it comes to broken marriages, most husbands will split the blame—half his wife's fault, half her mother's.
- Your ulcer can't grow very fast while you're laughing.
- If you must be blue, for goodness' sake make it a bright blue.

- Noah was the first businessman mentioned in the Bible. He floated a company at a time when the rest of the world was under liquidation.

- If anything makes a child thirstier than going to bed, it's knowing you've gone, too.

- An *eccentric* is a crackpot with money.

- A new toy is the perfect gift for the annoying kid next door—an electric train with sixty miles of straight track.

- The trouble with remaining calm these days is that people suspect that you must be onto something.

- A thing is not necessarily true because a man dies for it.

- Mistakes aren't so bad. Columbus found America by mistake.

- The more you try to eat your cake and have it too, the crumbier it gets.

- You are getting old when you get winded on the escalator.

- They say that many married folks are extremely happy, but the saddest thing in life is an absent-minded husband with a present-minded wife.

- A lasting gift to a child is the gift of a parent's listening ear—and heart.

- The family that stays together probably has only one car.

- We often wonder if the reason government costs too much is because we have too much government.

- The temptation to say an unkind word should first be rehearsed to see how it sounds when addressed to you.

- When some people get high, they feel mighty.

- A gossip is one who puts two and two together and gets four more than anybody else.

- Can you remember when a "drug problem" was nothing more than not being able to pay the drug store bill?

- With all the pollution in our streams today, all bridges are over troubled waters.

- Fast transportation has made us all neighbors—but, unfortunately, not brothers.

- Most politicians periodically mend their fences so it will be more comfortable when they straddle them.

- The opportunity of a lifetime must be grasped within the lifetime of the opportunity.

- It's strange how important your job is when you ask for a raise—and how unimportant it becomes when you want a day off.

- A modern version of the Mother Goose story: "There was an old woman who lived in a shoe. She had so many children, her monthly welfare check was $836.24."

- If we could see ourselves as others do, we'd simply think there was something wrong with our eyes.

- A man can steer a straight course and still be on the wrong side of the street.

- Why do some people make the same mistake time after time, when there are so many new ones they could be making?

- Sign in a swanky restaurant in Casper, Wyoming, Sure We'll Cash Your Check If You're over 80 and Accompanied by Your Parents.

- Most people put on weight in certain places—such as dining rooms.

- What keeps most would-be investors out of the stock market is the supermarket.

- Did you hear about the backsliding church member who attended church occasionally to discount his blessings?

- Wives are now reporting that husbands are unpredictable. They never know what story they'll tell them next that they're not going to believe.

- If push-button warfare is anything like push-button elevators, we'll wait a long time for it to arrive.

- One of life's briefest moments is the time between reading the sign on the expressway and realizing you just missed the exit ramp.

- When a man proposes on his knees, it sometimes takes him years to get back on his feet.

- The latest income tax form has been greatly simplified, consisting of only three parts: (1) How much did you make last year? (2) How much have you got left? (3) Send amount listed in (2).

- Police records show that no woman ever shot her husband while he was doing the dishes.

- One of the happiest men today is a vegetarian studying the prices in a meat market.

- Life is like a cafeteria. One goes through, choosing as he goes; but what he chooses must be paid for at the end of the line.

- The president has asked us to cut down on our use of power. Many people are asking the president to do likewise.

- Before deciding to retire from your job, stay home a week and watch daytime television.
- The toughest thing for some people to say in twenty-five words or less is *good-bye*.
- Any highway speed is okay, as long as you don't get caught or killed, whichever comes first.
- The best time to put kids to bed is very late—when they're too tired to fight back.
- Some men say they got married because they were tired of going to the laundromat, eating in restaurants, and wearing socks with holes in them. Other men get divorces for the same reasons.
- Science has increased our life span. We can look forward to paying our taxes at least ten years longer.
- A wise man is known by the smart things he doesn't say.
- Everybody should get at least a high-school education—even if he already knows everything.
- A three-foot clown recently married a five-foot, eight-inch showgirl. After the ceremony the guests threw rice—long rice for the girl, minute rice for the groom.
- Anyone who has trouble keeping his head above water probably isn't on his toes.
- The campaign to make horseback riding more popular has had widespread results.
- Most men close their eyes when they ride a bus. They hate to see women standing.
- The worst thing about accidents in the kitchen is that you usually have to eat them.
- A wealthy bachelor is just a guy who saved up his money to get married, and then changed his mind.
- Your spine is a long, limber bone. Your head sits on one end, and you sit on the other.
- It's not hard to pick out the best people. They'll help you do it.
- Why is it that the man who has nothing to say says it, while the man who does, doesn't?
- One reason the pioneers made good time crossing the country was that they didn't stop at souvenir shops along the way.
- A guaranteed hair-restorer is now on the market. The manufacturer gives a comb with every bottle.
- To profit from good advice requires more wisdom than to give it.

- When you hear that a man is going places, it means either that he's ambitious or his wife is out of town.
- Drive carefully! If motorists would give more ground, there'd be fewer in it.
- If and when you put your best foot forward, be sure to have your pet corn covered.
- Steaks are now so tough that you have to tenderize the gravy.
- A gasoline station in Iowa offers the extra touch with a sign that reads, Maps Refolded Here.
- Women like silent men. They think they're listening.
- It's a wise man who knows whether he's fighting for a principle or defending a prejudice.
- After a man has climbed high on the ladder of success, some of his friends begin to shake the ladder.
- Don't prepare so thoroughly for rainy days that you can't enjoy today's sunshine.
- If we could see ourselves as others see us—we'd probably look the other way.
- The constitution of the United States gives us the right to do our own thinking. It's up to us to acquire the ability.
- By the time a man understands women, he's no longer interested.
- The main discomfort in being a middle-of-the-roader is that you get sideswiped by partisans going in both directions.
- We may reduce highway speed just to save a few drops of fuel—a thing we would never do to save a few lives.
- At a certain age some people's minds close up—they live on their intellectual fat.
- Inflation is fantastic—people you once wouldn't give two cents for are now three for a quarter.
- A nutritionist in India has the perfect new diet food. You open a can, and there's nothing in it.
- Even the price of being poor today has gone up at least 20 percent.
- Tact is the art of building a fire under someone without making their blood boil.
- With all the wonderful new hearing aids being devised by science, it's a shame there aren't better things to hear.
- Have you heard about the bright young student who won a full scholarship to the college of his choice? It paid tuition, books, and bail.

- Many objections to law arise from the impossibility of making them apply only to the other fellow.
- Scientists tell us that the moon throws back radio waves from the earth—and we certainly don't blame it.
- She wasn't old—but when she lit the candles on her birthday cake, six people passed out from heat exhaustion.
- A young man in New Hampshire says his family often gets very religious—his father says "grace" before every meal and his mother says "Amen!" when the football game is over.
- At today's prices, we can't blame anybody for crying over spilled milk.
- Democracy is a remarkable system. It permits you to vote for a politician and then sit on the jury that tries him.
- It's probably not true any more, but a southern governor once explained why he welcomed visitors to his state, "One tourist is equal to a bale of cotton, and much easier picked."
- The way food prices are going up, more people are being put on diets by their accountants than by their doctors.
- Charity begins at home and winds up in foreign countries.
- You only have to mistreat a fellow a little to make him think it's a lot.
- No accurate thinker will judge another person by what that person's enemies say about him.
- The student of truth keeps an open Bible, an open dictionary, and an open mind.
- Work, of course, is the cure for unrest, but there are lots of people who think the remedy is worse than the disease.
- The nice thing about dictating a letter is that you can use a lot of words you don't know how to spell.
- If you think your automobile is expensive to operate, try a shopping cart.
- A pessimist is a fellow who turns out the light to see how dark it is.
- Knowledge becomes wisdom only after it has been put to practical use.
- A defeated candidate is another man who doesn't believe that the majority is always right.
- Humor is like a needle and thread—deftly used it can patch up just about everything.
- The biggest kitchen hazard facing the housewife preparing dinner nowadays is frostbite.

- Intuition is what tells a wife her husband has done something wrong even before he thinks of doing it.
- Things we don't need always seem to make us the happiest.
- The secret of happiness sometimes depends on what you don't do.
- Diplomacy is the art of letting someone else have your way.
- It must be a problem for two-faced people to put their best face forward.
- What this country needs is a credit card the Internal Revenue Service will honor.
- Some of our greatest bounces are the result of the fall that pride went before.
- Meeting the other person halfway would be much more satisfactory if we had a better idea of distance.
- It's hard to get a child to pay attention to you, especially when you're telling him something for his own good.
- *Personality* is what you are when lots of people are around. *Character* is what you are when everybody goes home.
- If this is the "soaring seventies," will we have the "aching eighties" next?
- The most cruel thing a parent can do these days is to push a bright child through school too fast. What if he arrives in college too young to grow a beard?
- If you are satisfied with little in yourself, how can you demand much from others?
- One reason it's often difficult to coax men to go to church is that men aren't interested in what other men are wearing.
- Someone described a bore by saying, "He reminds me of a toothache I once had."
- A woman can have both a career and a home if she knows how to put both of them first.
- The truth hurts—especially on the bathroom scales.
- People used to say, "It's not the cost—it's the upkeep." Nowadays it's both.
- Age is the best possible fire extinguisher for flaming youth.
- Streaking is a little like politics. The whole idea is to run and not get caught.
- Church is where you go to find out what your neighbors should do to lead better lives.

- Mankind has learned how to do a lot of things in the last hundred years—especially how to waste more.
- If you don't care how soon you're dead, keep driving through the red.
- A timid man said to his wife, "We're not going out tonight and that's semi-final."
- At least talk is still cheap. Unless, of course, it's with a psychiatrist.
- Sign on an office desk, Lead, Follow, or Get out of the Way.
- Good, like truth, is the same yesterday, today, and forever.
- The best way to appreciate your job is to imagine yourself without one.
- They are called "personal loans" because if you miss a payment they sure do get personal.
- Gasoline prices are so high! A man in Missouri recently drove into a station and asked for a dollar's worth of gasoline. The station attendant dabbed a few drops behind his ears.
- All husbands are just about alike, but they have different faces so you can tell them apart.
- You don't have to touch a live wire to get an electric shock. Just open your monthly bill.
- Nothing beats love at first sight except love with insight.
- If exercise is so good for you, why do athletes retire at about age thirty-five?
- There are three things that a man never gets back—his youth, his hair, and change from a ten-dollar bill at the supermarket.
- This is the time of year when the fellow who worked so hard to graduate wonders what the hurry was.
- It is reported that many resort hotels have towels so thick and fluffy that you can hardly close your suitcase.
- A New Mexico husband complains that his wife has two closets full of "nothing to wear."
- Cab drivers in Seattle have organized a football team. They call it the Taxi Squad.
- Your body is the baggage you must carry through life. The more excess baggage, the shorter the trip.
- A high-pressure salesman in Indiana is so convincing that he's now making a fortune selling a burial suit with two pairs of pants.

- People who are carried away by their own importance seldom have far to walk back.
- If you ask enough people you can usually find someone who'll advise you to do what you were going to do anyway.
- A flea circus may be a good act, but it takes termites to really bring the house down.
- The easiest in-laws to get along with are often someone else's.
- Middle age is that time of life when you convince yourself it's only a vitamin deficiency.
- When a man is generous, sometimes the last one to find it out is his wife.
- An operation is something that took a surgeon an hour to perform and a patient many years to describe.
- Being popular is a do-it-yourself job.
- Prices in some restaurants are so high now that you'd be wiser to watch your steak than your hat and coat.
- Kids are now so tough in the big cities that they no longer use bunnies for Easter—they use porcupines.
- Tolerance gets a lot of the credit that belongs to apathy.
- You can usually tell what makes a man tick when he's unwinding.
- Can you remember when the only real shortage we thought about was the miniskirt?
- Early to bed and early to rise makes your girl go out with other guys.
- April 16 of each year is the day you sit down and count your blessings—because nothing else is left.
- No wonder politicians pass the buck—it's now worth only fifty cents.
- Some drivers have slow reflexes—they don't know what lie to tell when they're getting a ticket.
- The way prices and taxes are soaring, the good old days were last week.
- We all have strength to endure the misfortune of others.
- Even with inflation, money still talks, but it carries on a cheap conversation.
- Some eat to live, others live to eat, and still others wish they could afford either.
- The biggest need in auto safety is to recall a few million defective drivers.

- There's nothing tighter than next year's budget or this year's bikini.
- On some freeways you can drive for miles and not leave the scene of the accident.
- We are living in an age of specialization. Even small apartments have two janitors—one to listen to complaints and one to ignore them.
- A hick town is a place where it's a lot easier to resist temptation than it is to find it.
- Most people don't object to criticism—if it's favorable.
- Judging by the high cost of eggs, somebody must have told the hens how much a bricklayer gets for laying brick.
- The trouble with running away is that mirrors are the same everywhere you go.
- In life we eventually learn that there is a speed limit in the pursuit of happiness.
- The page of instructions on the income tax form is a religious experience—it passeth all understanding.
- In the old days we were told to think about the future; but if a fellow stops to think these days, the future is already here.
- Many people learn by doing and by being done.
- The easiest shoes to fill are probably loafers.
- Many supervisors are office locomotives. All they do is run back and forth, smoke, and whistle.
- Fashion designers for women's clothing aren't running out of ideas—they're running out of material.
- People are guided to heaven more by footprints than by signposts.
- *Democracy* is a word all public men use and very few seem to understand.
- You get fed up in a restaurant these days just looking at the menu.
- One good thing about golf—a man doesn't get into any holes he can't get out of.
- Attention girls: Always save a boy friend for a rainy day—and another one in case it doesn't rain.
- A bigamist is a chap who has had one too many.
- An expressway is a highway with three lanes—a right lane, a left lane, and the one you're trapped in when you see the exit.
- Old quarterbacks never die, they just fade back and pass away.

- A man in Washington, D.C. declares he's enforcing consumer protection at the source. He's taken his wife's charge cards away from her.

- Junior brought home what is now remembered as his Watergate report card. First, he denied there was one; then he couldn't find it; but when he finally located it, three grades had been erased.

- If you want to keep your teeth in good condition, brush them after every meal and mind your own business.

- We have learned to fly through the air like birds; we have learned to swim in the water like fish; now we must learn to walk on the earth like men.

- A chronic liar is punished greatly in this life. He is not believed even when he speaks the truth.

- As an educational device, TV rates above everything else. No nation in history has ever known as much as we do about detergents and deodorants.

- There is plenty of room for everybody in this world—but we can't all have front rooms.

- A botanist is a man who knows all about flowers; a florist is a man who knows how much people will pay for them.

- Don't always think you're on the right road just because it is well traveled.

- People with an ax to grind often fly off the handle.

- It is difficult to view any man as a complete failure when you realize that he will probably brush his teeth more than 45,000 times during his lifetime.

- We can't understand how some women find the time to have their faces lifted. Most of us don't have the time to raise our eyebrows.

- Just about the time your income reaches the point where food prices don't matter so much—calories do.

- Adolesence is the awkward age when a child is too old to say something cute and too young to say something sensible.

- The guest who keeps saying he must be going doesn't mean it any more than the host who asks, "What's your hurry?"

- If an exception proves the rule, then two exceptions would be double proof.

- An ingrate is neither *in* nor *great*.

- If a man doesn't know where he's going, there is no telling where he'll be when he gets there.

- All the world's a stage, and some of us are getting stage fright.
- Many a man's idea of charity is to give unto others the advice he can't use himself.
- Historians tell us the past. Economists tell us the future. Only the present in confusing.
- It's possible to possess too much. A man with one watch knows what time it is. A man with two watches is never sure.
- People in other countries are not really rude, they are just trying to imitate some of our American tourists.
- The only thing thicker than some sideburns is what's between them.
- While the government reports that the average American is twenty-eight, the television industry still insists he's around seven.
- A man promised his wife $500 if she'd stop smoking cigarettes—and she did. Now he's offering her $1000 if she'll stop talking about it.
- The fellow who coined the phrase "What goes up must come down" certainly didn't have prices in mind.
- A politician in Arkansas reports that he has just concluded a very pleasant campaign. He only kissed the babies old enough to vote.
- Quite often, the bigger the shot, the smaller the caliber.
- It's a weird world. The strong take it away from the weak, the clever take it away from the strong, and the government takes it away from everybody.
- A woman usually underestimates two things—her age and how long it'll take her to get ready.
- To market, to market / my groceries to buy / home again, home again / to sit down and cry.
- About the only good thing about these withholding taxes is that a fellow doesn't get so mad all at one time.
- The average American home is so modernized that the only thing left to wash by hand is the kids.
- A politician is a man who gets sworn in and then cussed out.
- It's a great deal easier to make a mistake than to unmake one.
- A young woman in Montana complains that she's been trying to learn how to play golf all year, and all she's learned so far is how to drive a golf cart.
- The collapse of character often begins on compromise corner.

- A person isn't educated unless he has learned how little he really knows.
- No matter how limited your vocabulary is, it's big enough to let you say something you'll regret later.
- Man is a peculiar animal who can read the handwriting on the wall only when his back is up against it.
- Credit keeps a fellow from knowing how much past broke he is.
- When you see how willingly some young men go to the marriage license bureau, the idea of an all-volunteer army doesn't seem far-fetched.
- If you would like to have more people follow the straight and narrow path, stop giving them advice and start leading the way.
- No one can explain why children these days grow up sooner and remain children longer than ever before.
- Nothing makes you doubt you're as young as ever quite so much as trying to prove it.
- If a hen knew the current price of eggs, she wouldn't cackle—she'd crow!
- Folks would enjoy us more if we gave as much thought to our own behavior as we do to our neighbor's.
- You're getting older when all sports leave you tired—including just reading about them.
- For every person fearing the dark, there are ten afraid of the light.
- The most embarrassing moment of your life was when you spit out of a car window when it was not open.
- You have to admire the man who can still be enthusiastic about scientific progress after he has been caught speeding by radar.
- Every time the government shifts a little to the left, the decimal point in taxes and the national debt shifts to the right.
- Well-bred people never stir their coffee with their right hand. They use a spoon.
- Dreaming is often the only time you meet a better class of people.
- The mayor of a small Texas town remarked in his speech, "We are planning a new jail soon, and expect to be in it before the end of the year."
- You can't go about giving folks a piece of your mind without eventually being called empty-headed.

- A Tennessee husband gave his wife the following instructions when teaching her how to drive his car, "Go on green, stop on red—slow down when I begin to turn white."
- All these miracle drugs sound so good we sometimes feel sorry for ourselves because of our good health.
- Once upon a time there was a politician so honest that he was never investigated; so a group got together to investigate *that*.
- It's remarkable that cold feet are often the result of burnt fingers.
- Marriage also offers on-the-job training.
- You can't lose your head without losing your face.
- Some people's idea of roughing it is to spend a vacation in a town where they can get only one channel on a TV set.
- The undertaking business has its points. No matter how bad the service, the customer is in no condition to complain.
- We are all like eggs—we either hatch or go bad.
- In youth we run into difficulties. In old age difficulties run into us.
- The Society for the Elimination of Exclamation Points was recently formed. Its members consist of those people who are no longer surprised at anything.
- You'll have to give some folks credit for one thing—they can always think up a new crisis when the old one starts to play out.
- A small gift will do—if your heart is big enough.
- Some TV comics are like cracker jacks—half nuts and lots of corn.
- The lower politics goes, the higher it comes.
- No woman objects to being called intelligent, provided she's assured that it has done no harm to her looks.
- Being insulted by an enemy doesn't hurt a person nearly so much as being slighted by a friend.
- They continue to tell us that they are going to do something about "junk mail," but they keep on sending out income tax blanks.
- More and more lovely courtships sail into the sea of matrimony and finally sink in the rocky storms of divorce.
- Middle age, to our dismay, is when we are done before the day is.

- Sign on a church bulletin board in Benton, Winconsin, For God So Loved the World That He Didn't Send a Committee.
- A good listener is one who can give you his full attention without hearing a word you say.
- These days there are more tire tracks than footprints on the sands of time.
- Regardless of where some folks go for their vacation, about all they know when they get there is that they are there.
- It's a good thing that politicians can't live up to their promises. If they did, it might ruin the country.
- People with tact have less to retract.
- Three things are good in small measure and bad in large measure: yeast, salt, and hesitation.
- Many restaurants are now listing their hash on the menu as, Today's Conglomerate.
- In a small-town Wyoming newspaper, they list obituaries under "Civic Improvements."
- When a man climbs the ladder of success, we hope he remembers to thank those who held it for him.
- We've given our youngsters too much, too soon, and now it's too late.
- The world's problems are getting so complex that even the cab drivers and teen-agers no longer have all the answers.
- The happiest miser on earth is one who saves his friends.
- A hothead seldom sets the world on fire.
- Anyone who is plugged into current events is bound to be shocked.
- We fall the way we lean.
- It takes more courage to repent than to keep on sinning.
- The best thing a man can do is to help his wife correct his faults.
- Many convictions are usually family hand-me-downs.
- A woman wrote her ex-husband the following note, "Dear John, I hate you. Love, Mildred."
- To be a successful politician, find out where the public is going, take a short cut across the field, get out in front, and make them think you're leading the way.
- Another thing marriage brings out in a lot of men is silence.
- Some churches are filled with "retired" Christians.

- There is only a very thin line between being mature and over-ripe.
- Summer is Mother Nature's answer to the energy shortage.
- Bragging is delivering a *youlogy*.
- If you couldn't get another Bible, what would yours be worth?
- Frustration is not having anyone to blame but yourself.
- The yeast that raises the cost of living is inflation.
- When your out-go exceeds your income, then your upkeep will become your downfall.
- Sign in the window of a New York City laundry, We Do Not Tear Your Laundry with Machinery. We Do It Carefully by Hand.
- Working kills few folks, but worrying about having to work doubtless shortens the lives of many.
- A weather forecast is a program in which it takes fifteen minutes to say something that should be covered in ten words.
- Skiing is one major sport where success involves starting at the top and working your way down.
- There's a growing suspicion that what the world needs now is a religion that will cover the other six days of the week.
- By the time you know what it's all about, it's about over.
- Will someone please step forward and answer the following question: Why is it so much easier to believe something bad than something good?
- A woman's slacks are usually what makes us wonder why they aren't called something else.
- A Texan just back from a trip west reports he left his heart in San Francisco, his wife in Reno, and his bankroll in Las Vegas.
- Trouble defies the law of gravity. It's easier to pick up than to drop.
- Football builds self-discipline. What else would induce a spectator to sit out in the open in subfreezing weather?
- Television is great. We should all be proud to go blind watching it.
- People with one-track minds often have derailed trains of thought.
- Age is what makes furniture worth more and people worth less.
- Have you noticed that people who've stopped smoking and drinking haven't stopped talking about it?

- *Recession* is when the man next door to you loses his job. *Depression* is when you lose your job. *Panic* is when your wife loses her job.

- A national politician refuses to answer any questions on the grounds that it might eliminate him.

- It's comforting to see how much of what we failed to do wasn't worth doing anyway.

- One reason a pessimist isn't liked is that he so often has the opportunity to say, "I told you so."

- In Hollywood the average person's idea of a happy marriage is the next one.

- Some men play a fair game of golf. That is, if you watch them closely.

- A youthful figure is what you get when you ask her age.

- Lowbrows use "cuss words." Highbrows use "expletives."

- Some people think the moon won't be able to support life. Well, it's not so easy on earth either!

- A 1940 class reunion has the same old faces but a lot of new teeth.

- Some folks drink liquor as though they want to be mentioned in *Booze Who*.

- Statistics show that men who kiss their wives good-bye in the morning live five years longer than those who don't. Some of you men had better pucker up before you tucker out!

- There is one thing you can always be sure of—there will always be more people going on a diet tomorrow than those who have gone on a diet today.

- Many men are doing well in TV today. They have great faces for acid-indigestion commercials.

- It's quite true that money isn't everything, but it does come in handy when you've misplaced your credit cards.

- For fixing things around the house, nothing beats a man who's handy with a checkbook.

- A beautiful young woman in Maryland described her lover as follows, "He is old enough to be my father, but he's rich enough to be my husband."

- Abraham Lincoln had great difficulty getting an education—but what can you expect from a guy who didn't play football or basketball?

- There's a difference between "You look like a breath of spring" and "You look like the end of a hard winter."

- It might be possible for the straight and narrow road to be broadened a little if more people would walk it.
- Our country is in worse condition than we think—every time we call Dial-A-Prayer, we get a busy signal.
- The head usher to happiness is a well-kept conscience.
- Using cheap material to save money is like stopping the clock to save time.
- Nothing makes a storekeeper less cheerful than cheerfully refunding your money.
- Supermarkets are very convenient—they permit a shopper to go broke in one store.
- Why do they call it "going on a bender" when what actually happens is that one gets absolutely stiff?
- There's no such thing as a little trouble—if you're the one who's in it.
- Each year they make income tax forms easier to fill out and harder to pay.
- A fool and his money have a lot of fun while they are being parted.
- Many a standing ovation has been caused by someone jumping to his feet in an effort to beat the rest of the audience to the parking lot.
- Heavy drinkers have what is known as *saloon arthritis*—every night they get stiff in a different joint.
- Here's a good way to reduce the number of mistakes you make at work: Get there late and leave early.
- One of the sure signs of autumn is the tearing up of roads that should have been repaired during the summer.
- The hardest thing about gardening is getting out of doing it.
- People take heart when you give them yours.
- A continuing arms race can end the human race.
- The new weather satellites are great scientific improvements. It now takes the weather bureau only half the time to give the wrong forecast.
- If some TV shows are not taken off the air, the public will demand longer commercials.
- Love is an unusual game. There are either two winners or there are none.
- A middle-aged man in Vermont was heartbroken by unrequited love. He died of a broken liver.

- The most desirable quality of a nose is not its length, breadth, or curve, but that it not be found in other people's business.
- No matter how much conditions change, we tend to go right on doing as we have always done.
- Most of us have experienced an energy crisis for many years —we can't get going in the morning.
- At the entrance of Yellowstone Park is a sign, It's Not Nice to FOUL Mother Nature.
- No-fault insurance is nothing new. It's never been anybody's fault.
- A lot of people didn't foresee the coming of the automobile. Be careful crossing the street or you can still be one of them.
- If George Washington never told a lie, what is his picture doing on a dollar bill that's worth about forty-three cents?
- A gadget ceases to be a luxury the day your neighbor gets one.
- Old age has overtaken a man when he has to run to go as fast as he used to walk.
- An optimist sees the doughnut. A pessimist sees the hole. The realist eats it.
- Once our national sport was baseball. Now it's oddball.
- If you think habits aren't strong, try shaving the other side of your face first.
- A San Francisco woman says she's allergic to fur. Every time she sees a friend in a mink coat, she gets sick.
- The electric computer saves a man a lot of guesswork—but so does a bikini bathing suit.
- We all love a good loser—if it isn't us.
- One of the best ways to deaden a toothache is to walk into a dentist's office.
- The trouble with some people who don't have much to say is that they have to listen so long to find that out.
- Maybe these movies with so much violence should be shown in black and blue.
- Folks who think they know it all are amusing to those of us who do.
- Every bartender knows that one of the symptoms of someone who is tight is a loose tongue.
- The best time to end your speech is when you feel the listening is lessening.

- Sometimes a smile happens in a flash, but the memory of it often lasts forever.
- Politicians build campaigns on platforms, but some planks are too weak to stand on.
- A woman makes up her mind and her face several times a day and is seldom satisfied with the results of either.
- Americans have always been able to handle adversity bravely and successfully, but prosperity does us in.
- Don't forget that appreciation is always appreciated.
- You can tell who handles money in families nowadays—they're making women's handbags bigger and men's wallets smaller.
- Soft footsteps in the night mean that one of the kids is at the cookie jar again.
- Anyone with normal blood pressure these days just isn't paying attention.
- A college doesn't give you knowledge, it just shows you where it is.
- The nearer the time comes for our departure from this life, the greater our regret for wasting so much of it.
- If you think you can, or if you think you cannot, you are probably right.
- A politician will promise to do anything—just as long as he isn't expected to do it *now*.
- About the only satisfaction that comes from being broke is that it enables you to deal decisively with investment salesmen.
- Air travel is wonderful. It lets you pass motorists at a safe distance.
- There's a married couple in Idaho who are so concerned with their health that whenever they have an argument, she jogs to her mother.
- A *night owl* is a fellow who doesn't give a hoot about what time he gets in.
- Often what you don't say tells folks more about you than what you do say.
- Many people don't start economizing until they run out of money.
- A wise man's prayer, "Oh God, give the world common sense, beginning with me."
- There's a lot to be said for moderation in all things, but most of us would rather say than do.

- Gasoline scarcity makes walking healthier—and fewer cars to dodge.
- The average shopping cart will hold one kid and a week's wages.
- Where you live makes a difference. The fellow known in the city as a dashing playboy is known in a small village as the town drunk.
- The most obsolete term in the English language is *tax-free.*
- We can stand a guy's gift of gab—if he picks up the luncheon tab.
- Thousands of people will not be going on vacation this year. In fact, many of us can't even afford to stay at home.
- Perpetual motion can be found in almost any committee meeting.
- Beware of the man who keeps telling you he's on your side. So is appendicitis!
- Most of us wouldn't mind Uncle Sam's bite—if he didn't keep coming back for dessert.
- A bore only stops talking to see if you're listening.
- It is better to take things as they come than to try to catch them as they go by.
- The Lost and Found Department is where people bring things they've found and can't use.
- Things sure get confusing these days. This year Washington's birthday was February 18. Last year it was February 19, but George and his mother always thought it was February 22.
- A devoted husband is one who assures his wife each morning that she's right.
- If we could use the money political candidates spend on their campaigns, we could cure a lot of the ills they complain about.
- The handwriting on the wall usually means you're in a telephone booth.
- Travel agency sign in Galveston, Please Go Away.
- When was the last time you walked by a furniture store that wasn't having a sale?
- Freedom is a package deal—with it come responsibilities and consequences.
- People who depend on their family tree for status had better shake it first.

- Divorce in on the increase and so is alcoholism. A lot of folks whose marriages are broken are apparently throwing themselves on the mercy of the quart.

- Anything that is easier said than done can usually be done a great deal easier if so much wasn't said.

- Telephone service is getting worse. Now you must dial twice just to get the wrong number.

- A person isn't necessarily stubborn when he doesn't take your advice.

- One reason photographs don't always look natural is that photographers always tell their subjects to look pleasant.

- Men come of age at sixty, women at seventeen.

- Many a person is credited with being brave when in fact he didn't have sense enough to recognize danger.

- Unhappiness is not knowing what we want and killing ourselves trying to get it.

- You can always tell when a man is dining out with his wife—he always counts his change.

- Our national anthem tells us that this is the land of the free—the Internal Revenue Service proves it isn't.

- Most of us agree that it is human nature to think wisely and to act in an absurd fashion.

- If prices continue to rise, there'll be more marriages ending in bankruptcy than in divorce.

- The recipe for perpetual ignorance is to be satisfied with your opinions and content with your knowledge.

- A debt collector is not as unpopular as some people think. Almost everybody asks him to call again.

- It's better to construct the future than to varnish the past.

- All the great things are simple, and may be expressed in single words: freedom, honor, duty, mercy, hope, and love.

- Do you know the difference between a beautiful woman and a charming one? A beautiful woman is one you notice; a charmer is one who notices you.

- Inflation is an economic situation which occurs when the prices you get look good and the prices you pay look awful.

- What is it about human nature that makes it easier to break a commandment than a habit?

- The most difficult thing to explain is something you had no business saying in the first place.
- Some public speakers are guilty of podium pollution.
- It's a pity there isn't a pesticide available for controlling the litterbug
- A person becomes wise by observing carefully what heppens when he isn't.
- Modesty is the art of bragging inconspicuously.
- It is reported that many people in the past enrolled for a memory course—and then forgot why.
- The old-timer remembers when both panhandlers and restaurant owners asked for a nickel for a cup of coffee.
- A worker in Illinois says he has a very responsible job—when anything goes wrong, he's responsible.
- The time a father worries most about his son is when he remembers what he was doing at this age.
- Modern woman has a lot of problems, and she thinks she can solve most of them by yelling at her husband.
- The hardest train to keep on the track is the train of thought.
- A little learning is a dangerous thing if you think it's a lot.
- Windy debates by politicians are like bass drums—after you listen to both sides you still haven't heard much.
- Any patient can tell you that nowadays a hospital bed is the closest thing to a parked taxi with the meter running.
- The expedient thing and the right thing are not always the same.
- It is almost impossible for you to sink somebody else's boat and still keep your own afloat.
- Trouble is what gives a fellow his chance to discover his strength—or lack of it.
- If economic conditions continue as they are now, a typical week of the future will likely include a Meatless Monday, Heatless Thursday, Gasless Sunday and Bankless Payday.
- A short cut is usually the quickest way to some place you weren't going.
- There are girls who are still single because they couldn't stay awake while some guy talked about himself.
- It will be interesting to hear the teen-agers of today tell their children what they had to do without when they were young.
- Many people are not pessimists—they're merely discontented optimists.

- Can you remember way back when the early bird got the worm? With daylight saving time, he can't even see it.

- A good pipe is as great a comfort to a man as a good cry to a woman.

- You are slightly past middle age if, before you step off the curb, you look down once more to make sure the street is still there.

- The best place for a woman to hide her age is in the nearest beauty parlor.

- If it takes all kinds of people to make a world, it looks as if there are still some we haven't got.

- The voter has only one consolation—not every candidate running for office can be elected.

- A prominent Russian newspaper announces that it is running a contest for the best political joke. First prize is twenty years.

- You know you've put on too much weight when you try to loosen your belt—and you can't find it.

- One trouble with our country is that the stupid people are sure of everything, and the intelligent ones are full of doubt.

- A father in Ohio described his teen-age son, "He looks like the victim of a hit-and-run haircut."

- If you are willing to admit that you are all wrong when you are all wrong, then you're all right.

- Marriage entitles a woman to the protection of a stalwart man who'll hold the ladder while she paints the ceiling.

- At any banquet you'll find more after-dinner speakers than after-dinner listeners.

- An apple a day keeps the doctor away—an onion, everybody!

- More boys would follow in their father's footsteps if they weren't afraid of being caught.

- Installment buying seems to be here to stay—but a lot of things bought that way aren't.

- Surgery can really take something out of a person.

- Dieting is the time when the days seem longer and the meals seem shorter.

- God created the energy; we created the crisis.

- Hard work and devotion to duty will surely get you a promotion— unless, of course, the boss has a relative who wants the job.

- A glutton is someone who still has an appetite after seeing today's prices.

- Men and money are much alike—the tighter they get, the louder they talk.
- Common sense in an uncommon degree is what the world calls wisdom.
- Even if you can't prevent another's sorrow, caring will lessen it.
- A hick town is where a man is known by his first name and last scandal.
- Ignorance is not the problem. It is not knowing when we are ignorant that causes the difficulty.
- Honesty is like an icicle. If it once melts, that's the last of it.
- There may be fewer cars on the road, but the number of nuts driving them hasn't diminished.
- He who laughs last didn't get the joke.
- The noisier a fellow gets, the less likely we are to listen to him.
- Smart folks lose their temper permanently.
- It seems like this country would be better off if businessmen had more orders from customers and less from Washington.
- An old-timer is one who recalls when Home Brew was the favorite malted milk of the flivver set.
- Meat prices these days can put you in a stew.
- It's easy to smile when someone cares.
- Many people know how to make a living. Few know what to do with it when they have it made.
- The best way to keep teen-agers home is to make their surroundings pleasant—and let the air out of the tires.
- Pollution is so bad in St. Louis that a drum majorette threw her baton in the air—and it stuck.
- Television is with us to stay—if we can keep up the payments.
- The new income tax form is printed in red, white, and blue. When you've filled in the white, you're left in the red, and that makes you blue.
- In Hawaii, where the weather is the same the year round, we wonder how they start conversations!
- People will always take you at your own valuation—if you downgrade yourself.
- Sometimes a man goes to Las Vegas out of curiosity and comes home out of funds.
- Now that it's behind you, what did you do yesterday that you're proud of today?

- Inflation is like getting stuck in a traffic jam. You find you are a part of the problem, but you can't figure out what to do about it.

- Some rights are worth dying for. The right-of-way is not one of them.

- Wouldn't it be wonderful if we could force the recall of all Form 1040s?

- About all the exercise some people get is pulling ice trays out of the refrigerator.

- Be grateful for your bad habits. If it weren't for them, you wouldn't have anything with which to make New Year's resolutions.

- It's hard to teach kids the alphabet these days. They all think *V* comes right after *T*.

- Traffic tickets are like wives. No man complains about them until he gets one of his own.

- More people are flattered into virtue than bullied out of vice.

- Bumper sticker on a car in Tyler, Texas, Read the Bible—It'll Scare Hell out of You.

- For the holidays, why not give the gift that keeps on giving—a female cat.

- A gentleman in Nevada looked at his supermarket bill and announced, "Never before have so many given so much for so little."

- What this world needs is someone smart enough to foretell the future, then change it before it happens.

- All some people want is their fair share—and yours, too.

- Nothing makes resisting temptation easier, than another more attractive temptation.

- A typical Christmas in Reno is when everybody gathers around the slot machines and sings carols.

- The most useless thing in the world is gossip that isn't worth repeating.

- Wouldn't it be wonderful if all those who point a finger would hold out a friendly hand instead?

- With some men, financial security means getting lifetime jobs for their wives.

- Egotism is that certain something which enables a man who's in a rut to think he's in the groove.

- Nowadays, we're divided into three groups—the haves, the have-nots, and the charge-its.

- What's the use consulting a doctor for a cold if it gives you heart trouble when you get the bill?
- A couple in Colorado report they have a happy marriage—now and then.
- There are many paths to the top of the mountain, but the view is always the same.
- Charm is the ability to make someone else think that both of you are quite wonderful.
- Unexpressed ideas are of no more value than kernels in a nut before it has been cracked.
- The only loafer who makes money these days is a baker.
- If you don't rest as much as your doctor tells you, he says you're uncooperative; if you rest more than he advises, he says you're lazy.
- Many of our modern girls have plenty of polish—on their fingernails.
- Laugh and the world laughs with you; cry and the other guy has an even better sob story.
- If Diogenes wandered about seeking an honest man today, chances are he'd exclude Washington from his itinerary.
- Columbus discovered America for only one reason—he wanted to give Europe a place from which to borrow money.
- A doctor in Milwaukee turned kidnapper but failed because nobody could read the ransom note.
- Everyone should have at least two friends—one to talk to and one to talk about.
- Bulletin board notice in Minneapolis, Conserve Energy—Work Slower.
- Someone has come up with a novel Christmas Club idea—you save up to pay for last year's gifts.
- A Hollywood actress is always talking about her last picture or her next husband.
- Gossip is like grapefruit. In order to be good, it has to be juicy.
- A twentieth wedding anniversary is difficult to celebrate. It's too soon to brag and too late to complain.
- Anybody who doesn't feel insecure these days is probably living in some remote, uncivilized corner of the world.
- A spinster is someone who can't understand why any girl would want an unlisted phone number.

- Some folks use mighty weak thread when they start to mend their ways.
- It's hard for a fellow to stumble onto something good while sitting down.
- Since the advent of sex education, the old fellow who drives the local school bus can't tell whether the kids are talking dirty or discussing their lesson assignments.
- The energy situation is getting so bad that even rumors are traveling slower.
- You can't take it with you because at today's prices you're in the hole before you get there.
- Washington, D.C. is so divided that highly-placed insiders aren't even talking to authoritative sources.
- Without the draft, a lot of fellows are going to think up some other reason not to get married.
- There is more pleasure building castles in the air than on the ground.
- The only people you should want to get even with are those who have helped you.
- An elderly gentleman in Georgia says he drinks whiskey for medicinal purposes only—and wore out three tablespoons in a single year.
- There is always a right way and a wrong way, and the wrong way usually seems the more reasonable.
- Most husbands become interested in politics. In fact, many of them are already the minority leader in their house.
- There's so much air pollution that people are coughing even when they're not in church or watching a movie.
- In the old days, if a man missed the stagecoach, he was content to wait a day or two for the next one. Nowadays he feels frustrated if he misses one section of a revolving door.
- The most difficult arithmetic to master is the art of counting our blessings.
- Nothing makes folks bird watchers faster than pigeons.
- As many people gave up smoking cigarettes this year as last —and a lot of them were the same people.
- No woman lives long enough to try all the recipes she clips out of the newspapers and magazines.
- It's funny how a bad cold improves enough to let you accept a party invitation.

- The dollar has dropped in value—but there's no need to worry until some country turns down our foreign aid.
- A busy executive told an aide, "I have to make a speech on the Ten Commandments—please give me a brief resume."
- When a kid hears a bad word, it goes in one ear and out his mouth.
- Seven steps to stagnation: "We tried that before." "It costs too much." "We've never done it that way before." "We're not ready for that." "That's not our responsibility." "We're doing all right without it." "It won't work."
- Reading the happenings of the day one wonders how it is possible for so many adults to have so little maturity.
- One of the easiest things to find in any office or shop is fault.
- People who diet go to great lengths to avoid great widths.
- To bear fruit most grapevines, trees, and speeches need pruning.
- There's a new item available guaranteed to reduce the cost of living. It's a smaller shopping cart.
- Courage is what it takes to stand up and speak; courage is also what it takes to sit down and listen.
- The way of the transgressor may be hard—but it sure isn't lonely.
- Men have split the atom, broken the sound barrier, and landed on the moon—but watch them trying to sew a button on a shirt.
- We should be happy living in a country where we put chains on tires and not on people.
- A bargain is anything that looks better than it is and sells for less than it was.
- Nothing is harder to see than the naked truth!
- On the tombstone of a window washer who plunged to his death, Gone With the Windex.
- When it comes to mink coats, some women will go to any lengths—half, three-quarters, or full.
- It looks like today's modern car won't start until the seat belt is fastened—and the pocketbook is emptied.
- There are so many credit cards in use today that the only people with cash are kids who just got their allowance.
- Baldheaded people should remember that when God made heads, He covered up the ones He didn't like.
- Television is like the toaster—you press a button and the same thing pops up most of the time.

- Some people suffer in silence louder than others.
- Bank interest on a loan is so high now that if you can afford to pay it, you don't need the loan.
- How often have you met a critic of the church who has tried to make it better?
- It pays to preserve your peace of mind. It's just about the only peace that you can find.
- Good human relations is nothing more than treating people as if it were their last day on earth—not yours.
- Unless you are willing to admit your ignorance, you will never be able to acquire knowledge.
- A safety belt is an item motorists use religiously for ten minutes after they've passed an accident.
- One thing the discovery of the North Pole revealed was that there is nobody sitting on top of the world.
- The three Rs used to be readin', 'ritin', and 'rithmetic. Today, they are rioting, rebellion, and restlessness. If this continues, we'll have regret, rot, and ruin. What we need is respect, religion, and responsibility.
- A beautiful heart more than offsets the handicap of a homely face.
- The United States is the only country in the world where a man can keep three cars in his garage and not own a single one of them.
- There are two kinds of people in Las Vegas—the haves and the used-to-haves.
- Marriage is sometimes just a ceremony in which two people promise from now on they won't lie to anybody but each other.
- The more sure you are, the more wrong you can be.
- People worry most about two things these days. One, that things may never get back to normal; and, two, that they already have.
- We keep asking God to bless America. He already has, now it's our turn.
- Most kids think a balanced diet is a hamburger in each hand.
- These days the only thing that gives you more for your money than it did a year ago is a bathroom scale.
- Adolesence is when you think you'll live forever. Middle age is when you wonder how you've lasted so long.
- Note on a mail package, Fragile. Throw Underhand.

- A woman doesn't usually check up on her husband. Unless, of course, she doesn't know what he is doing.

- To be seventy years young is sometimes more cheerful and hopeful than to be forty years old.

- Psychologists say that no person should keep too much to himself. As long as the Internal Revenue Service is around, nobody is likely to do so.

- Why is it that many men who wouldn't commit larceny will steal a busy man's time?

- One of the surest marks of good character is a man's ability to accept personal criticism without feeling malice toward the one who gives it.

- The automobile has certainly discouraged walking—particularly among pedestrians.

- More lies have been told about spinach than about fishing.

- A parent in Kentucky decided he had better attend the PTA meeting after he received a note from one of his children's teachers, "Pleze kum to our parint-tee-chers meeting."

- Eat, drink, and be merry—tomorrow they may recall your credit cards.

- The trouble with socialism is that when people lean on one another too much, they soon get too weak to stand alone.

- Inflation is when you find your nest egg won't even make an omelet.

- George Washington had a problem no president since has had to deal with—he had no previous administration to blame for his troubles.

- A husband and wife in Omaha report they are doing their best to ease the fuel shortage—they've cut out their heated arguments.

- Biting remarks are often the result of snap judgments.

- We always hear of "old-fashioned honesty"—but dishonesty has quite a long genealogy, too.

- People usually feel they have reached forty prematurely.

- It's often a show of strength not to show strength.

- Most of us could do twice as much if we didn't spend half the time explaining why we don't.

- We keep trying to find new ways to improve the quality of life—while neglecting the ways we already know.

- The older generation thought nothing of getting up at 6 A.M. The younger generation don't think much of it either.

- Some politicians campaign for the funds of it.

- A man in Mississippi was told that most accidents happen within twenty miles of home—so he moved to another town fifty miles away.

- Generally speaking, a baby sitter is a teen-ager who behaves like an adult while the adults are out behaving like teen-agers.

- We can keep up with the Joneses—it's the Smiths that bug us.

- A New Mexico bride says she can't get used to being whistled for instead of at.

- The most talk-about people at a family reunion are those who didn't show up.

- A fellow doesn't have to do wrong to be mistreated. He only has to appear to do wrong.

- The gift some people appreciate most is something you made yourself—such as money.

- Conscience is what keeps giving you minority reports a majority of the time.

- It is better to be silent like a fool than to talk like one.

- A friend is one who strengthens you with his prayers, blesses you with his love, and encourages you with his hope.

- No girl ever met a perfect man she didn't try to improve once they were married.

- Many men switch from golf to bowling—because they don't lose near as many balls.

- The easiest way to get a teen-ager to be quiet is to ask him where he's been when he gets home.

- Nowadays it's around the cloverleaf, over the bridge, and through the viaduct to grandma's house.

- If a fellow is stubborn and successful they say he has *perseverance*; if he is stubborn and unsuccessful, he's *obstinate*.

- The first step toward divorce is getting engaged.

- A man is worth no more than he esteems himself.

- Some people treat life like a slot machine—putting in as little as possible while hoping for the jackpot.

- A smart secretary takes shorthand at arm's length.

- It's strange how much better our memory becomes as soon as someone borrows money from us.

- The only thing that's perfectly understandable about some modern paintings is the price tag.

- A woman shopper asked a perfume counter clerk, "What do you have that'll compete with three hours of baseball on TV?"
- Some businessmen consider their budgets balanced if they can afford to buy stamps to mail out their bills.
- All things come to him who hustles while he waits.
- In certain parts of the world people pray in the streets. Over here they are known as *pedestrians.*
- The trouble with some health foods is that you have to be healthy to screw the lid off the jars.
- Inflation is getting so bad that even people who don't plan to buy anything are griping about prices.
- One can almost become rich by hoarding—or you can become happy by sharing.
- There is no acceptable substitute for honesty; there is no valid excuse for dishonesty.
- Anybody who's walking on clouds is apt to be carried away.
- Happiness is a healthy mental attitude, a grateful spirit, a clear conscience, and a heart full of love.
- Many of us think that life would be so much more enjoyable if we didn't have to work our way through it.
- Some people's vacation calls for two *weeks* or two *thousand*—whichever comes first.
- There are times when the truth is not extremely kind.
- Good intentions die unless they are executed.
- The most difficult years of marriage are those following the wedding.
- Engines are lubricated with oil, human hearts with kindness and love.
- Maybe women don't practice sleight of hand, but how do you explain that so many twist their husband around their finger without letting him know it?
- The world is full of trouble; but so long as we have people undoing trouble, we have a pretty good world.
- A man isn't really poor if he can still laugh.
- Food has gotten so high you can hardly stomach it.
- The new bikinis make women look better and men look longer.
- A lie is the deliberate withholding of any part of the truth from someone who has the right to know.
- The TV reruns will begin when summer begins—including weather forecasts.

- Acrobats are able to turn a flop into a success.

- A small boy in Jacksonville said to a grocery clerk, "Here's my dime, I'll take a piece of penny candy."

- The secret of writing is to learn the big words—and then learn not to use them.

- A slap on the back doesn't always mean encouragement —mosquitoes get it too.

- Some girls can't take a joke, but others prefer one to no husband at all.

- Life is pretty tough—but think how much tougher it would be if we didn't sleep away one-third of it!

- The main hope of civilization is that people may get together some day and try it.

- Maybe it's because love makes you dizzy that people say it makes the world go round.

- Time invested in improving ourselves cuts down on time wasted in disapproving of others.

- If you're always in hot water, at least you don't have cold feet.

- The fact that the world was created in six days shows what could be done before we had coffee breaks and wage-and-hour laws.

- When your education is finished, you are.

- Juvenile delinquency would disappear if kids followed their parent's advice instead of their example.

- If the Lord had meant for us to be on our toes all the time, He wouldn't have given us so much on which to sit down.

- You can't always be right, but you can do your best at all times—and that is what counts.

- Fabulous wealth and fame awaits the man who designs a woman's shoe that's bigger on the inside than it is on the outside.

- Seems like the only things that are on the up and up in Washington is the Washington Monument and the Capitol dome.

- Many a man has lost his job, not because they had a reason to fire him, but because they didn't have any reason for keeping him.

- As a rule, the best things are done by a committee of one.

- People who live together without being married are making a big mistake. They'll never know the thrill of a divorce.

- A bath mat is a little rug that children like to stand beside.

- Sign in a garage, Don't Smoke Here. If Your Life Isn't Worth Anything, Gasoline Is.
- Nothing makes an argument so one-sided as telling about it.
- Tomorrow is two days too late for yesterday's job.
- In most marriages the husband is the provider and the wife is the decider.
- Counter-strategy is keeping your elbow out of the other fellow's coffee.
- After sixty-five every birthday is alike. You just look forward to reaching it.
- Any man who correctly guesses a woman's age may be smart—but he's not very bright.
- Sarcasm is the curdled cream of wit.
- A habit is something a fellow hardly notices until it is too strong to break.
- Fishing is the art of doing almost nothing.
- If the Internal Revenue Service gave green stamps, thousands of people would look forward to paying their income tax.
- Weather forecasting is still a few hours behind arthritis.
- There is an enormous difference between *hearing* and *listening*.
- A man gains polish through the daily grind.
- Unfortunately, to most nations "ironing out differences" usually means shooting irons.
- Men, like zippers, work better after a little soft soap.
- You don't realize you're buying gold bricks until you get an estimate on a new house.
- If ignorance is really bliss, we'd all be a whole lot happier.
- Tax collectors are funny folks. They expect a fellow to give them the money he's already spent for something better.
- A good executive is one who can make decisions quickly—and sometimes correctly.
- The one letter in the alphabet that causes us the most concern is *i*. We don't worry much about *u*.
- You will find that if you share your brother's burden, both of you will walk straighter.
- When a man sees eye to eye with his wife, it's a sure indication that his vision has been corrected.

- A city-dweller who just moved to the suburbs said the most beautiful sound the first week was the birds chirping. The most annoying sound was the second week of birds chirping.

- Love looks through a telescope; envy through a microscope.

- How-to-get-rich books are now filed under *Fiction*.

- A gossip is one who can turn an earful into a mouthful.

- The trouble with square meals is that they make you round.

- It's easier to love your enemies if you remember that they never try to borrow from you.

- The man who rolls up his sleeves seldom loses his shirt.

- A hypocrite is a person who writes a book praising atheism —and then prays that it will be a good seller.

- If a man can see both sides of a problem, you know that none of his money is tied up in it.

- The trouble with a woman forgiving and forgetting is that she keeps reminding you that she's doing it.

- A hair in the head is worth two in the brush.

- The love of money is the root of all evil—and it is also the root of most industry.

- A family circle can't be kept intact with a triangle.

- Summer is a time when breadth is more noticeable in short pants.

- It is when men stop having faith in one another that they stop having faith in their government.

- Every Amercian is entitled to the pursuit of happiness—at a pace under fifty-five miles an hour.

- Our favorite attitude should be gratitude.

- Two hundred dollars used to be the down payment on a car; now it's the sales tax.

- Nothing makes a man faster on his feet than politics—unless it's bigamy.

- Destiny may shape our ends, but our middles are our own choosing.

- When a middle-aged woman still has her school-girl figure, it probably wasn't much to begin with.

- It's gotten to where a lot of folks who itch for money won't scratch for it.

- Free advice can be costly.

- Let us hope we can take our vacation before postcards go up again.
- Most failures were experts at making excuses.
- Getting out of compact cars is like having debts—it takes time to get straightened out.
- If you take your wife out to dinner, the tax department won't let you put it on the expense account—meaning you can't deduct for entertaining the boss.
- In almost any restaurant a "rare steak" is one that costs less than five dollars.
- To experience something is to have lived it.
- It seems that the main idea of TV is to provide as cheaply as possible something to fill in between those expensive commercials.
- Sign in a cafeteria, Our Silverware Isn't Medicine—It's Not to Be Taken After Meals.
- There is a shortage of raisins—even grapes refuse to grow old and wrinkled.
- Some tax loopholes become nooses.
- God never tires of hearing from us in prayer.
- The woman who thinks no man is good enough for her may be right—and then again, she might also be left.
- Forty is the age when you begin to realize how much fun you had when you were twenty.
- Anyone who thinks there is a shortage of coins hasn't been to church recently.
- It looks like the only folks trying to hold back inflation are the folks selling girdles.
- Politicians who walk straight run better.
- A "rare gift" is any kind a woman gets from her husband after ten years of marriage.
- It's wonderful to grow old—if you can remember to stay young while you are doing it.
- Be kind to unkind people—they probably need it most.
- Education is a wonderful thing. If you couldn't sign your name, you'd have to pay cash.
- Thousands of people are afraid of the unknown—and also of many parts of the known.
- When your wife hangs on to every word you say, she probably wants to see if your story will hold together.

- One good thing about being human is that it's something so many of us have in common.
- Many people would like to be respected without having to be respectable.
- It would be a lot easier to lose weight and keep it off if the replacement parts weren't so available in the refrigerator.
- We don't mind people telling us the way it is if they're willing to do something about the way it ought to be.
- Inflation is prosperity on the rocks.
- Why is it that wisdom arrives with old age—too late to do us much good?
- If you can separate good advice from bad advice, you really don't need any advice.
- While many observers dispute the popular belief that American men spoil their wives, they don't say who does!
- People are giving worthless papers to universities and calling it a tax-deductible gift. Other people are giving worthless, worn-out clothes to the needy and calling it charity.
- A fellow ought to live so that anyone speaking against him will be recognized as a liar.
- It's hard, if not impossible, for a politician to keep envy out of his voice when he accuses his opponent of fooling the people.
- All a protest march proves is that there are some people who are still able to walk.
- We are only young once. This is all society can stand.
- The quickest way to stop gossip is for everybody to shut up.
- When you see some people work, you wonder what they'll do when they retire!
- The United States now faces another crisis—trying to tell the boys from the girls.
- At least these days you don't have to worry about getting more than you bargained for.
- The most painful operation a person can undergo is the cutting off of his credit.
- Kids are learning so much in school these days that some of them are as smart as their parents say they are.
- The wages of sin are apt to include a lot of overtime.
- If all the world's a stage, it's about time for a new plot.
- Most people talk the way they think—but more often.

- Most new cars have so many warning lights and buzzers around the dashboard that just driving one makes you feel nagged to death.
- The problem that baffles Washington is how to dig the country out of the hole without making the hole any bigger.
- Folks ought to appreciate daylight saving time because after paying all their taxes, time may be all they have left to save.
- It's easier to climb the ladder of success if your daddy made the ladder.
- Inflation proves that Columbus was right—the world *is* flat.
- When two women used to get together, they'd talk about another woman; now, they talk about supermarket prices.
- The most disappointed people in the world are those who want everything that is coming to them—and get it.
- It doesn't seem such a hardship to have to do without something that the neighbors can't afford either.
- Now we know why they call politics the most promising of all careers.
- A well-informed man is one whose wife has just told him what she thinks of him.
- People who invite trouble always complain when it accepts.
- We're afraid the boys in Washington think our foreign policy is an endowment policy.
- More than 15 percent of all tornadoes occur in June. That's when most marriages occur too.
- Finance is the art of passing currency from hand to hand until it finally disappears.
- Pity your boss. He has to come in early to see who comes in late.
- The idea of housework to a modern girl is to sweep the room with a glance.
- American motorists take fine care of their cars—and they keep pedestrians in good running condition, too.
- Children never put off until tomorrow the things that will keep them out of bed tonight.
- A brilliant young law student in a western state reports that he has learned that an oral contract is not worth the paper it is written on.
- Making good in America should include helping to make America good.

- Most people are willing to change, not because they see the light but because they feel the heat.
- The man or woman who marries for money usually earns every penny of it.
- If you want to follow in your father's footsteps, don't wear loafers.
- One good thing about the good old days—if you bought a horse, you could be sure the model wouldn't change next month.
- It looks like common sense ain't as common as it used to be.
- Advertisement for a loan company, We Take the Moaning and Groaning out of Loaning.
- Almost every American home has all kinds of labor-saving devices but very few money-saving devices.
- The best cure for a short temper is a lengthened prayer life.
- Barnum said many years ago that there's a sucker born every minute. Thanks to automation, production seems to have been stepped up.
- If a fellow can't be a runner-up, he should try not to be a runner-down.
- Never exaggerate your faults—leave that for your friends.
- Crossing the street is perfectly safe. It's not quite making it that's dangerous.
- Nothing makes you feel so cheap as giving yourself away.
- In Washington they're either tapping the phones or tapping the till.
- Thanksgiving Day is when some are more full than thankful.
- Nothing makes a woman feel older than meeting a bald-headed man who was two grades behind her in school.
- A Georgia girl reports that she didn't want to marry her boy friend for his money—but there didn't seem to be any other way to get it.
- Middle age is the awkward period when Father Time starts catching up with Mother Nature.
- The reason talk is cheap is because the supply is plentiful and the demand is slight.
- A politician described his opponent as "a sneak who'll promise you two cars for every family—then, after he's elected, he'll put in more parking meters!"

- If you think getting an education is expensive, try not getting one.
- There are a lot of good books telling you how to manage when you retire. What most people want is one that'll tell them how to manage in the meantime.
- The fellows who used to stand around the corner candy store are all grown up and married. Now you'll find them hanging around the laundromat.
- A little white lie soils very easily.
- The secret of success: Never let down and never let up.
- A "sensational new idea" is sometimes just an old idea with its sleeves rolled up.
- Everyone wishes to have the truth on his side, but it is not everyone who wishes to be on the side of truth.
- Fools live to regret their words, wise men to regret their silence.
- It is not the body's posture but the heart's attitude that counts when we pray.
- A transistor radio is a noisy plastic case with a teen-ager attached.
- Any man who says he can read a woman like a book is probably illiterate.
- It's true that you can't fool all the people all the time—but some highway signs come pretty close.
- Attention public speakers: Nothing can be said after thirty-five minutes that amounts to anything.
- A meteorologist is one who has more scientific aids than you have in guessing wrong about the weather.
- We should learn silence from the talkative, toleration from the intolerant, and kindness from the unkind.
- Advertising is what tells us which luxuries we can't do without.
- Any man who is honest, fair, tolerant, charitable of others, and well behaved is a success no matter what his station in life.
- Some church members are so busy with their church work they don't have time to practice their religion.
- Knowledge has to be improved, challenged, and increased constantly or it vanishes.
- The only way to avoid bad habits is to make it a habit to avoid them.
- What a nice world this would be if we loved others as we love ourselves!

- A flood is nothing more than a river that has gotten too big for its bridges.

- The easiest way to make relatives feel at home is to visit them there.

- About 50 percent of the married people in this country are glad they didn't remain single—and all of them are women.

- A good friend is like toothpaste—comes through in a tight squeeze.

- Eat, drink, and be merry, for next month it will probably cost you 6.2 percent more.

- Football is popular with girls. They like to see men making passes.

- There should be a special watch for taxpayers. It wouldn't tick—just wring its hands.

- The experienced parent is one who has learned to sleep when the baby isn't looking.

- A man is not necessarily smart just because he says things that smart.

- Note to gluttons: Don't forget that what's on the table eventually becomes what's on the chair.

- The greatest wonder of this modern age is wondering what will happen next.

- Never bite the hand that feeds you. The chances are it's your own.

- May good fortune follow you all the days of your life—and finally catch up with you.

- Pressure is what most college kids major in, but nobody studies.

- Paranoia is when a person imagines people are staring at him as if he invented income tax.

- You should teach a child to wait on himself—even if you're married to him.

- The key to a happy retirement is to have enough money to live on but not enough to worry about.

- Advice is what you get when you're not going to get anything else.

- Heavy whiskey drinkers get 50 percent more cavities than milk drinkers—but they go to the dentist in a much better frame of mind.

- Insincere praise is worse than no praise at all.

- Sometimes the best way to convince a man he is wrong is to let him have his own way.

- If you are disgusted, frustrated, and upset about your children, just imagine how God must feel about His!

- Honesty is not only the best policy, it is rare enough today to make you pleasantly conspicuous.

- A man of stature does not need status.

- About all a thin dime will buy you these days is a thin stamp.

- The scales of justice have long been overbalanced by excessive waits.

- If you can't help worrying, remember that worrying can't help you either.

- You can't see straight if you've got "I" trouble.

- A road map is what some motorists use to find out how they got where they are.

- Christ was one child who knew more than His parents—yet He obeyed them.

- Organized labor is now publishing a new magazine called *Time And A Half*.

- A walk down main street should convince anyone that today's forgotten man must be the barber.

- You must "fill the pulpit" if you wish to "fill the church."

- It is possible that you could stop an army of a million men, but you can't stop a right idea when it comes along.

- Marriage means sharing half of the groceries with someone else in order to get the other half cooked.

- Juvenile delinquency is like charity—it begins at home.

- It's easier to open the door of opportunity after you have a key position.

- Actually, the fountain of youth can be found in the hallways of any elementary school.

- People and things change; principles and facts never change.

- Early to bed and early to rise makes a man healthy, wealthy —and apt to get his own breakfast.

- A bargain is something that would cost a lot more if you had any use for it.

- Anybody who throws his weight around seldom has his feet on the ground.

- A deficit is what you have when you don't have as much as you would have if you didn't have anything.

- After much insistence on her part, the parents gave their co-ed daughter a new car as a birthday present. On the windshield was a card signed, "With all our love, mama and pauper."

- It's one thing to itch for something but quite another thing to scratch for it.

- The bedfellows politics makes are never strange. It only seems that way to those who have not watched the courtship.

- An executive knows something about everything; an expert knows everything about some things; and a switchboard operator knows everything.

- The only time where ends meet now is on a football field.

- A man with feelings wields more power than a man with muscle.

- An antique is usually something people forget to throw out until it becomes valuable.

- When a married man dreams he's a bachelor, it means he's going to be disappointed when he wakes up.

- Sign outside a cemetery, Owing to Employment Difficulties, Grave Digging Will Be Done by a Skeleton Staff.

- Lukewarmness is to be decent but not dedicated, comfortable but not committed.

- Folks are so easily deceived that most of us deceive ourselves.

- We pity any person of ninety who reached it with nothing more to show than how pleased he is to have reached it.

- About all a divorce does is to give a couple a chance to make the same mistake twice.

- A lot of people are going to do something about air pollution as soon as they can see their way clear.

- It's true that opposites attract. For example, a lot of hard cash often winds up in soft hands.

- The favorite dish of every housewife is one that's just been washed and dried.

- A man is a selfish fool when he says it's nobody's business what he does.

- So-called rock singers have the kind of voice that belongs in silent films.

- It's strange how people always announce they're going on a diet *after* a big meal, never before.

- No child is apt to respect the thing his father ridicules.

- A bore doesn't stop talking even when you've stopped listening.

- The vice-presidency is like the last cookie on the plate. Everybody says he won't take it, but someone always does.
- Soup should be seen and not heard.
- The easier a girl is to look at, the harder a man looks.
- Television is what gives you nothing to do when you aren't doing anything.
- The greatest mistake you can make in this life is to be continually fearing you will make one.
- If you think you work harder than the average worker, you're an average worker.
- The only person worth envying is the person who doesn't envy.
- To succeed, keep your head up and your overhead down.
- Make each day count, but don't count each day.
- Old Dame Rumor must be mighty tired—she has been working overtime lately.
- Twenty-nine is a wonderful age for a man to be—and for a woman to stay.
- The best thing about some men is their wife.
- Nothing makes a man the boss of the house as much as living alone.
- In the world where plants communicate by the wave lengths of their fragrance, we'd guess that garlic is probably known as "old loudmouth."
- The next thing to being young and pretty is being old and rich.
- One ounce of sense will hide a pound of ignorance.
- Taxpayers are always hoping for a break in the levy.
- White House employees are no longer permitted to use the polite expression, "Pardon me."
- The stock market has been known to bring more people to their knees than all the preachers put together.
- Bumper sticker on back of a truck, Make Love, Not War. Stop Driver and Ask for Details.
- Adolesence is when children start bringing up their parents.
- A real family man is one who looks at his new child as an addition rather than a deduction.
- Why don't supermarket carts have brakes as a safety measure—brakes that would bring the cart to a screeching halt at, say, thirty-five dollars?

- There aren't many old-fashioned family doctors around because there aren't many old-fashioned families.
- An ulcer sometimes indicates that the owner is in the big money—either making it or owing it.
- A woman will go to almost any length to change her width.
- Please remember that when you eat in a fancy restaurant, the food will be plain—but the prices will be fancy.
- There are a great many has-beens in the world today, but there are probably more never-weres.
- Keeping up with the Joneses is no problem—it's paying up that causes the headaches.
- A man in Wyoming says he recently attended an interesting movie about Julius Caesar. When Caesar was stabbed, half of the audience left—they didn't want to get involved.
- There is a face-lift you can perform yourself that is guaranteed to improve your appearance. It is called a smile.
- It must be terrible for a girl to marry a man for life—and then learn he doesn't have any.
- Today's best labor-saving device is tomorrow.
- Christmas is a race to see which gives out first—your money or your feet.
- A political spellbinder is someone who can talk for hours without having to stop to think.
- Even in Hollywood they are having finincial trouble. Executives who used to pinch the girls are now pinching pennies.
- The last word in any argument is what a woman has. Anything a man says after that is the beginning of a new argument.
- There seems to be a consensus these days that the government is doing more *to* the average citizen than it does *for* him.
- It may take a magician to pull a rabbit out of a hat, but any old fool can let the cat out of the bag.
- Egotism is what makes other people *think* they're as intelligent as we *know* we are.
- A certain character in Oregon read that most accidents take place in airplanes and bathtubs—and hasn't been in either since.
- Some folks have no use for other folks they can't use.
- You can't expect a fellow to know right from wrong if he can't even tell bad from worse.

- Nothing makes unemployment so serious as not having a job.
- Marriage is a nice life for a man to lead—if only his wife would let him do a little leading.
- Most of our rock 'n' roll musicians should be plucking chickens instead of guitars.
- A vacationer just back from a long car trip says the trip could have been more enjoyable except for two things—the billboards and the board bills.
- Perhaps the only place people have no trouble making ends meet these days is on the dance floor.
- Memory is the faculty that enables you to give somebody most of your zip code.
- Greed has three facets: love of things, love of fame, and love of pleasure.
- In a recession, things cost too much to buy. In a depression, you can't buy things because you don't have enough money.
- Making an honest living should be an easy matter because there is so little competition.
- An election year is a period when all the Democrats and all the Republicans devote their time to saving the country from each other.
- A southern gentleman living in retirement says he's been playing golf—but only on days ending with y.
- We never thought we'd see the day when the neighborhood grocery took in more money than the neighborhood bank.
- The average girl is looking for a man clever enough to make a lot of money and foolish enough to spend it.
- People who know it all never learn anything.
- About the only way to get as much as ever for a dollar is to have it changed.
- The man who says his wife can't take a joke forgets that she took him.
- A doctor in Tulsa still makes house calls—he charges ten dollars a flight of stairs.
- One of the most difficult things to give away is kindness—it is usually returned.
- These days it's better to face the music than to have to listen to it.
- If opportunity knocked, some folks would pretend they were not at home.
- A homemade friend is a lot better than one bought.

- Will someone please step forward and explain why a woman will always look into a mirror—except when she's backing into a parking spot!

- The secret of being miserable is to constantly worry about whether or not you're happy.

- At one time if you paid cash, people figured you were thrifty. Today they figure your credit is no good.

- Adult education got its start in a household with teen-age children.

- The only thing easier to skin than a banana is a taxpayer.

- Bikini: the difference between not very much and nothing at all.

- The heaviest thing a person can carry is a grudge.

- Doubtless, 1974 will go down in history as the year when Watergate sprung a leak.

- What we need in this country is more open minds and fewer open mouths.

- Getting a husband or a wife is like buying an old house. You don't see it the way it is but the way you think it's going to be when you get it remodeled.

- Hardening of the heart affects more people than hardening of the arteries.

- The money from which a fool is soon parted won't stay with anybody else very long either.

- In the hectic confusion of modern society it would be nice to experience a few dull moments occasionally.

- The world would be a much nicer place if the busybodies could be persuaded to do nothing when there is nothing to do.

- It's incredible when you think about how little our parents knew about child psychology and how wonderful we turned out to be!

- Friends suspect that a recent marriage isn't going too well—he stays out all night, and she doesn't know it.

- You need to go on a diet if you find yourself puffing when walking down stairs.

- Ulcer victims are members of the fret set.

- A cynic says a phony is anybody who's better than you.

- Today's supermarkets are so big that you can go farther than your money.

- A recent retiree in Vermont writes that he's tired already: "I wake up in the morning with nothing to do, and by bedtime I have it only half-done."

- The average man has probably thought twice about running away from home—once as a child and once as a husband.

- Some foreign countries are considering placing a tax on American tourists—probably another way of trying to make them feel at home.

- The following ad recently appeared in a Baltimore newspaper, For Sale—Used Set of Barbells. Good Condition—Lifted Only Once.

- Recent discoveries indicate humans are at least 4 million years old. On Mondays some of us feel even older.

- The best time to give advice to your children is when they're young enough to believe all that nonsense you're telling them.

- Part of today's problem is that our paychecks are minus tax and our bills are plus.

- Playing golf is like raising children—you keep thinking you'll do better next time.

- You can suffocate a thought by expressing it in too many words.

- Always remember that it is better to give than to receive. Besides, you don't have to write thank-you notes.

- The evil that men do lives after them. If you don't believe this, watch a TV rerun.

- The government will soon conduct a survey as to why people get bored on the job. Just thinking about this report makes one drowsy.

- Doctors have noted that women's feet are getting larger. Presumably that's because they are trying to fill men's shoes.

- A young fellow in Indiana gave away his water skis—he couldn't find a lake with a slope.

- Sign on the window of a dress shop in Milwaukee, "Wedding Gowns for All Occasions."

- One of the recent political candidates still can't understand his defeat—he doesn't know if it was because he lied too much or too little.

- Retirement is when you sit around and watch the sunset—when you stay up that late.

- It is estimated that the FBI has over 70 million fingerprints in its files. So has every home containing small children.

- Folks keep saying that hard work never killed anybody, but, come to think of it, we never heard of anyone resting themselves to death.

- The greatest danger in bad times is bad remedies.
- Do you realize that if they still had debtor's prisons, this entire country would be behind bars?
- The best way to get along economically is to tighten your belt. That is, if you can afford a belt.
- It seems there are few things to laugh at these days, but the time to really worry is when this includes yourself.
- The people of this nation are sick of the high cost of being sick.
- Children's bedtime could be described as the storm before the calm.
- Some of these young fellows, whose mothers think they have a spark of genius, seem to be having ignition trouble.
- Men are luckier than women. If they are ugly, they can grow hair all over their face and no one knows the difference.
- When we hear a man boasting about how much liquor he can hold, we get a mental picture of an animated garbage can.
- American holdup men seem to get about everything except what's coming to them.
- An old-timer remembers when, if you mentioned dirty books in the library, you meant they were dusty.
- A man in Iowa says the first time he ever fell *up* was when he wore his new bifocals the first time.
- When someone complains about prices today, one thing is certain—he's buying, not selling.
- Maybe what this country really needs is a return to our original form of government—by the people.
- A husband knows his wife loves him when she returns a dress he can't afford.
- Interest your children in bowling—get them off the streets and into the alleys.
- A real friend is a person who asks you an important question to which you know the answer.
- Once upon a time it was hard to save money. Now it's difficult just to stay broke without going into debt.
- The handwriting on the wall usually means you're going to have a great deal of trouble getting it off.
- A woman shopper in Louisville reported to the police that a thief had stolen fifty dollars worth of groceries from her car—they took it right out of the glove compartment.

- Age is like love. It cannot be hid.
- The cost of living has risen so much that some merchants are thinking of moving their bargain basement up to the third floor.
- Criminals seem to know their rights better than their wrongs.
- A well-adjusted citizen these days probably has friends who wonder what's wrong with him.
- Not all stenographers look up words they're not sure of. Some can't spell that well.
- Don't try to cross a bridge until you're sure one is there.
- An Oklahoma man just back from Las Vegas says he took the "chef's tour" while there. He was baked in the sun, stewed at the bar, and burned at the crap table.
- Business is doubtless "sound," as the experts say, but at times the sound is a little mournful.
- A man's wife may not be the only woman he's ever loved, but she's the only one who made him put it down on paper.
- America celebrates its two-hundredth birthday soon, and all we've learned in that time is how to go fast, work less, waste more, and die quicker.
- People will believe almost anything you say if you whisper it and don't have bad breath.
- A nice man in New Mexico says his brother-in-law is so dumb that even stupid people notice it.
- It was reported that *Gone With the Wind* was so expensive to make that even the intermission cost a million dollars.
- A fellow recently out of the hospital says he learned what a disturbed patient is—one who just got his bill.
- Suburbia is where the houses are further apart and the payments closer together.
- There's a new organization called Wives Anonymous. You phone them and they will send someone over to talk your husband out of watching football on Sunday afternoons.
- A woman in New York City won a divorce when she charged that her husband made her unscrew the light bulbs to save wear and tear on the switches.
- The reason the cow jumped over the moon was because there was a short circuit in the milking machine.
- A bigot is a person who slams his mind in your face.
- Everything is so frantic nowadays that even if you want to relax you have to work at it.

- Some object to the fan dancer and others to the fan.
- Just about everybody will agree that our country is on the move, though there is plenty of argument about the direction.
- An American will cheerfully respond to every appeal except to move back in a bus.
- We hope they don't raise the standard of living any higher. We simply can't afford it.
- There is a town in Arizona so small that the north and south ends are on the same side of town.
- A businessman in Salt Lake City claims his secretary is tremendously efficient. She hasn't missed a coffee break in several years.
- Have you found a penny in the street recently? It was probably a dime when someone dropped it.
- Never give advice before you're asked—or after!
- We crucify ourselves between two thieves: regret for yesterday and fear of tomorrow.
- Having the right aim in life doesn't mean a thing if you're loaded with blanks or don't know when to pull the trigger.
- Every year it takes less time to fly across the Atlantic Ocean and longer to drive across town.
- At the present time there is no such thing as petty cash!
- Always get in the shortest line at the supermarket—in so doing you may get to the cashier before the prices go up.
- It's strange that nobody will listen to your advice unless you're a doctor or lawyer and charge for it.
- Nothing cures insomnia like the realization that it's time to get up and go to work.
- Some people are so stingy that when they go away for a week, all they spend is seven days.
- The worst thing about middle age is that you outgrow it.
- Wouldn't it be wonderful if folks tried as hard to find nice things to say about the living as they do about the dead?
- If opportunity came in the form of temptation, knocking once would be enough.
- Spoiled kids soon become "little stinkers."
- There is a school in a southern state so tough that the teachers play hooky more than the pupils.

- A certain college student explained that he was suffering from "financial surgery"—meaning his parents had cut off his allowance.

- When Congress tries to decide between two new taxes, it's like a woman deciding between two new dresses. She usually decides to take both.

- In the old days men stood up for women—but there were no buses then.

- Some folks can't even play solitaire without cheating.

- It's hard for a child to live right when he has never seen it done.

- The biggest obstacle to the return of the five-cent cup of coffee is the cost of water.

- Nowadays even chaos has almost become normal.

- The best things in life are free, of course, but isn't it a pity that most of the next best things are so expensive?

- A politician is a man who says, "Glad to see you again"—although he's never seen you before.

- Bumper sticker on old car, Don't Pass—PUSH.

- People who say they don't get all they deserve probably don't know how lucky they are.

- The difference between law and custom is that it takes a lot of nerve to violate a custom.

- A cynic in Pennsylvania says he treats his wife the same way that he treats other strangers.

- The battle of the sexes will have to be called off if it gets any harder for one side to identify the other.

- A slow eater eats less—particularly in a large family.

- One thing this country desperately needs is a grocery cart with four wheels that all go in the same direction.

- 1973 will always be remembered as the year when the dollar and the White House were devalued.

- Today when newlyweds feather their nest, you'll usually find four parents who have been plucked.

- If food prices keep going up, TV dinners will soon cost more than TV sets.

- The handiest item a housewife can have at her fingertips is a husband.

- Always remember that a man is not rewarded for having brains, but for using them.

- One reason marriages break up isn't because men don't understand women—it's because women don't understand football.

- Did you know that Las Vegas is unbeatable—the climate, the excitement, and the crap tables?

- Students who read lots of books are called bookworms. Now that they are taught by tapes, should we call them tapeworms?

- Trying to curb inflation by raising taxes is like giving a drunk another drink to sober him up.

- Excuses fool no one but the person who makes them.

- Nothing stretches slacks like snacks.

- Egotism is the anesthetic that deadens the pain of stupidity.

- How is it that we can look through the old family album and split our sides laughing—then look into the mirror and never even crack a smile?

- Double trouble is a mother-in-law with a twin sister.

- The reason old folks enjoy living in the past is because it's longer than their future.

- Lots of money uncovers a multitude of relatives.

- It is reported that someone recently broke into the Kremlin and stole next year's election results.

- There's one curve that looks as good on a man as it does on a woman—a smile!

- College years is the only vacation a boy gets between his mother and his wife.

- The thing we dread most about parking is the noisy crash.

- If you can't crown yourself with laurels, you can wreathe your face in smiles.

- You can tell an old movie on TV—it's when the doctor tells the patient, "You're as sound as a dollar."

- The best way to knock the chip off a fellow's shoulder is to pat him on the back.

- Social security is an old-age insurance system that guarantees you a steak after all your teeth are gone.

- It's easy to accept the fact that you're not worth your weight in gold. What's really shattering is not being worth your weight in pork chops.

- One thing a man learns from arguing with a woman is how to be a good loser.
- Congress fighting inflation is like the Mafia fighting crime.
- Anybody who tells you he never made a mistake is probably relying on a mighty poor memory—his or yours.
- Bureaucracy is based on a willingness to either pass the buck or spend it.
- Anything whispered or shouted usually isn't worth hearing.
- One of the nicest things about being bald is that when company comes, all you have to do is straighten your tie.
- A coordinator is a man who can bring organized chaos out of regimented confusion.
- The Russians often find the American way of life very confusing—so do Americans for that matter.
- Sign on a junior executive's desk, It's Not Whether You Win or Lose—It's How You Place the Blame.
- If you must go against your better judgment, do it when she's not around.
- If you were arrested for being kind, would enough evidence be found to convict you?
- Money is an ideal gift these days—everything else is too expensive.
- It's better we disagree, than agree and all be wrong.
- When a man "suffers in silence," it's most likely his wife's.
- A father who encourages his boy to follow in his footsteps has probably forgotten a few.
- There are two times when children will contradict you—when you're wrong and when you're right.
- Life's irony: We get bent from hard work and broke without it.
- A cease-fire is where the shooting continues but the outside world pays no attention.
- The best way to compliment your wife is frequently.
- Eagles on dollars are proper and right because they symbolize swiftness of flight.
- It's no trick to meet expenses—the toughest job is to avoid them.
- A person's handwriting reveals a lot about his character—especially when he has signed a check that bounces.
- You get out of life what you put into it. That's the trouble.

- The best time to take a cold shower is some other time.
- A store window sign in Jackson, Mississippi, Staying-in-Business Sale.
- We are sure that automation will never be able to replace the taxpayer.
- The tongue of some people is like a friendly dog's tail—always wagging.
- If Americans bought only what they could afford, it would destroy our economy.
- When will deodorant manufacturers end the under-arms race?
- There's a new diet that will reduce weight like nothing else. It's called the high price of food.
- Satisfaction is the best kind of internal revenue.
- Recession is when we get our clothes out of mothballs instead of out of clothing stores.
- Even old age doesn't creep up on you like Christmas.
- Apparently the government has abandoned the idea of abolishing poverty, investigation having shown it was the only thing left within reach of everybody.
- There are only two sure ways to avoid paying alimony—either stay married or stay single.
- People who do a lot of kneeling don't do much lying.
- Fairy tales used to start, "Once upon a time. . . ." Now they start, "When I am elected. . . ."
- The older a man gets, the farther he had to walk to school as a boy.
- Money isn't everything, but it does quiet the nerves a little.
- What the weatherman saves for a rainy day is probably an alibi.
- On his one-hundredth birthday, a salty gentleman in Georgia said, "If I'd known I was going to live this long, I'd have taken better care of myself."
- No matter how you order it, nowadays you get your steak served expensively.
- Nothing makes advice so helpful as giving it.
- Tact is the ability to make a person see the lightning without letting him feel the bolt.
- Americans will pay a big price for any invention that will help them save time they don't know what to do with.

- With phone prices going up, the dime will be useful only for what it was originally designed—a small screwdriver.
- A young kid kicked a store Santa saying, "That's for last year."
- Someone commented on a woman who got a big alimony settlement, "She lost the marriage but won the divorce."
- Middle age is when each day makes you feel two days older.
- Apparently the only thing that hasn't increased in cost is free advice.
- Maybe the reason the Las Vegas population is increasing is that more people don't have the money to leave.
- We may complain about the heat in the summer, but at least we don't have to shovel it.
- The sea of matrimony is where many a poor fish gets hooked with his own line.
- Everybody is willing to lend a helping hand to the fellow who has trouble opening his pocketbook.
- Don't throw mud. Even if you miss, your hands are still dirty.
- We don't have the right to complain about the mistakes made by people who are doing the work we should be doing.
- An open mind is wonderful if a mouth to match doesn't go with it.
- A miser might be pretty tough to live with, but he makes a nice ancestor.
- If some of these self-made men had it to do over again, they'd call for some help.
- How can the meek inherit the earth when there won't be any lawyers around to draw up the papers?
- When a person sells principle for popularity, he is soon bankrupt.
- A marriage seldom goes on the rocks when a couple finds something in common to laugh about. For instance, there's always the old wedding picture.
- There are two sides to almost every question, and if you wish to be popular you must take both.
- It's strange how much better our memory gets as soon as someone borrows money from us.
- The biggest problem most wives face is the one sitting across from her at the breakfast table.
- Profanity is the use of strong words by weak people.

- A doctor is a guy who tells you if you don't cut out something, he'll cut something out of you.
- Most women keep secrets like politicians keep promises.
- Politeness is offering a lady your seat when you get off the bus.
- A pessimist is a man who thinks everybody is as nasty as himself and hates them for it.
- Flattery looks like friendship—just like a wolf looks like a dog.
- Nothing seems to last as long as a pair of shoes that don't fit.
- Grocery bags seem to have gotten stronger. The bag that could hold ten dollars worth of food ten years ago now easily holds twenty dollars worth.
- Winter is like long underwear—it creeps up on you.
- A clever investment today is the one you didn't make.
- Many people, always talking about getting away from it all, have never been with it in the first place.
- It's hard to figure who does more bragging—those who've lost weight or those who've quit smoking.
- Politicians are all vegetarians—they are always interested in straw votes and grass roots.
- It's a pleasure to sit before a warm fire in the living room on cold nights—that is, if you have a fireplace.
- The reason many people drink booze is because they are always trying to cure a cold or prevent one.
- Some women have very little regard for husbands, especially if they already have one.
- Divorce seems to be going out of style—probably because marriage seems to be going out of style.
- Why not learn to enjoy the little things—there are so many of them.
- A political platform is something to get in on—then forget.
- Most of us have always been broke—all the recession did was to make it official.
- After listening to her husband's tirade, the wife remarked, "You may not have had a happy childhood, but you are certainly having a long one."
- No two people are alike—and both of them are glad of it.
- Inflation is when a man can lose his shirt in the supermarket as well as in the stock market.

- You never realize what a good memory you have until you try to forget something.
- The way most people live within their income is partly.
- Winter always seems long because it comes in one year and out the other.
- Temper is a valuable possession—don't lose it!
- Love is often a condition that warms the heart, quickens your pulse, and transplants your money.
- Sending your child to college is like sending your clothes to the laundry. You get out what you put in, but often you don't recognize it.
- Worry kills more people than work. Some play it safe by doing neither.
- You probably won't hear opportunity knock if the television set is always on.
- Everybody should have equal rights—even parents!
- To make a long story short, try long distance.
- There is a town in Idaho so small that the Barbershop Quartet is composed of two people.
- On New Year's morning, when you look in the mirror, what you see is what you regret.
- Medication is so expensive these days that doctors are giving prescriptions with a note: "Take one pill as often as you can afford it."
- Sign in a Palm Springs, California, high school, In the Event of an Earthquake, the Supreme Court Ruling Against Prayer in School Will Be Temporarily Suspended.
- The most easily breakable things in the world are promises.
- Once it was ambition that kept people on the move. Now it's No Parking signs.
- Some people who get credit for being patient are just too lazy to start anything.
- Business has been so bad at one major hotel that the management is now stealing the towels back from the guests.
- Food prices are so high that it's no longer possible to bite off more than you can chew.
- There's nothing as annoying as a neighbor who keeps the noise up and the shades down.
- Instead of turning over a new leaf as the old year ends, some folks ought to tear out a few back pages.

- One thing this country needs is fewer needs.
- If you would quit nursing that grudge, it might die.
- More unions would go out on strike for a living wage—but nobody seems to know exactly what that is.
- Some folks are so lazy that if their ship came in, they'd expect someone else to unload it for them.
- What you don't say about yourself says a lot about you.
- Gasoline shortages have always resulted from too much horsepower and not enough horse sense.
- Can you remember when day care centers were called *home*?
- We wonder why they call it the "rush hour" when folks cannot do any rushing because of the crowds.
- Nowadays "petty cash" is a fitting description of almost anybody's salary.
- The way the cost of living and taxes are today, you might as well marry for love.
- If you think a seat belt is uncomfortable, you've never tried a stretcher.
- Bumper sticker on a Chicago car, Save on Electricity. Move in with Relatives.
- When a woman driver puts on her directional signal, it probably means she's going to turn one way or another.
- TV commercials are educational. They teach you how stupid advertisers think you are.
- Alaska is larger than Texas—but it won't be when it melts.
- The devil finds work for idle hands. Now private industry needs to do the same!
- Proof that Americans are a tolerant people lies partly in the fact that the inventor of the juke box died a natural death.
- Husband hunting is probably the only sport in which the animal that gets caught has to buy a license.
- The great problem is that the key to success doesn't always fit your ignition.
- Things would be a lot nicer if antique people were valued as highly as antique furniture.
- You can always tell when you're on the right road—it's upgrade.
- No one has more faith than the person who plays a slot machine.

- Plaque on the desk of a New Orleans executive, Once I Thought I Was Wrong, but I Was Mistaken.
- Some people can always tell when it's Monday. That's the day after the day they forgot to go to church.
- Foreign dictators are hard to figure out. You can never tell whether they are smart men bluffing, or imbeciles who mean it.
- Women distrust men too much in general and not enough in particular.
- Commencement is when the collegian who learned all the answers discovers that there are a new set of questions.
- A mere layman can't understand why efficiency experts don't go into business for themselves and monopolize the world.
- The time will certainly come when we will learn that the heart can never be totally right if the head is totally wrong.
- It's a great pity that, because of the force of gravity, it takes more energy to close the mouth than to open it.
- An echo is pretty accurate, but it doesn't contribute very much that is new.
- The economist usually has a plan to do something with somebody else's money.
- Diplomacy is to do and say the nastiest things in the nicest way.
- A recent Hollywood marriage broke up so fast that the wife got custody of the wedding cake.
- Some men stay single because they don't understand women. Others get married for the same reason.
- Many people are so afraid of dentists they need an anesthetic just to sit in the waiting room.
- A fanatic is highly enthusiastic about something in which you are not even remotely interested.
- Florida is the state where the hurricane season isn't the only time there's too much wind blowing.
- Doctors can cut out most anything that is the matter with you nowadays except your foolishness. You have to cut that out yourself.
- A polite driver is one who sounds his horn before he forces you off the road.
- There's nothing as dull as going on the kind of vacation you can afford.
- God doesn't expect folks to solve all the world's problems—He only expects them not to create them.